Our Sufficiency In Christ

John MacArthur, Jr.

THOMAS NELSON
Since 1798

OUR SUFFICIENCY IN CHRIST

All Scripture quotations in this book, except those noted otherwise, are from the New American Standard Bible © 1960, 1962, 1963, 1968, 1971, 1972, 1973, 1975, and 1977 by The Lockman Foundation, and are used by permission. Those indicated NIV are from The Holy Bible, New International Version. Copyright © 1973, 1978, 1984 International Bible Society. Those indicated KJV are from the King James Version.

Library of Congress Cataloging-in-Publication Data
MacArthur, John 1939–
    Our sufficiency in Christ : how we have displaced our true spiritual resources with mysticism, pragmatism, and psychology / by John F. MacArthur, Jr.
        p.   cm.
    ISBN 0-8499-0840-X
            0-8499-3519-9 (tp)
    1. Spiritual life. 2. Christianity—20th century—Controversial literature. I. Title.
IN PROCESS (ONLINE)   91–8434
                                                                          CIP

Printed in the United States of America

3 4 5 9 LB 9 8 7 6 5 4 3 2 1

*To the memory of D. Martyn Lloyd-Jones,
a gifted servant of God, who in another place and
time built his life and ministry on the sufficiency
of Christ. May there be many more like him.*

In Him all the fulness of Deity dwells in bodily form, and in Him you have been made complete.

Colossians 2:9–10

CONTENTS

ACKNOWLEDGMENTS

Thanks to Phil Johnson, Dennis McBride, and
Lance Quinn, good friends whose contributions
to this effort are known to the Lord.

PREFACE

IN HIS BRILLIANT SATIRE *THE SCREWTAPE
Letters* C. S. Lewis imagined this dispatch from the demon
Screwtape to his apprentice, Wormwood, who was trying
desperately to keep his human "patient" from practicing
biblical Christianity:

> My Dear Wormwood,
>   The real trouble about the set your patient is living
> in is that it is *merely* Christian. They all have individual
> interests, of course, but the bond remains mere Chris-
> tianity. What we want, if men become Christians at all,
> is to keep them in the state of mind I call "Christianity
> And." You know—Christianity and the Crisis, Christi-
> anity and the New Psychology, Christianity and the
> New Order, Christianity and Faith Healing, Christianity
> and Psychical Research, Christianity and Vegetarian-
> ism, Christianity and Spelling Reform. If they must be
> Christians let them at least be Christians with a differ-
> ence. Substitute for the faith itself some Fashion with
> a Christian colouring. . . .

The use of Fashions in thought is to distract the attention of men from their real dangers. We direct the fashionable outcry of each generation against those vices of which it is least in danger and fix its approval on the virtue nearest to that vice which we are trying to make endemic. The game is to have them all running about with fire extinguishers whenever there is a flood, and all crowding to that side of the boat which is already nearly gunwale under. Thus we make it fashionable to expose the dangers of enthusiasm at the very moment when they are all really becoming worldly and lukewarm; a century later, when we are really making them all Byronic and drunk with emotion, the fashionable outcry is directed against the dangers of the mere "understanding." Cruel ages are put on their guard against Sentimentality, feckless and idle ones against Respectability, lecherous ones against Puritanism; and whenever all men are really hastening to be slaves or tyrants we make Liberalism the prime bogey.

But the greatest triumph of all is to elevate this horror of the Same Old Thing into a philosophy so that nonsense in the intellect may reinforce corruption in the will. It is here that the general Evolutionary or Historical character of modern European thought (partly our work) comes in so useful. The Enemy [God, in Screwtape's reckoning] loves platitudes. Of a proposed course of action He wants men, so far as I can see, to ask very simple questions; is it righteous? is it prudent? is it possible? Now if we can keep men asking "Is it in accordance with the general movement of our time? Is it progressive or reactionary? Is this the way that History is going?" they will neglect the relevant questions. And the questions they *do* ask are, of course, unanswerable; for they do not know the future, and what the future will be depends very largely on just those choices which they now invoke the future to help them to make. As a result, while their minds are buzzing in this vacuum, we have the better chance to slip in and bend them to the action *we* have decided on. And great work has already been done. Once they knew that some changes were for the better, and others for the worse, and others again indifferent. We have largely removed this knowledge. For the descriptive adjective "unchanged" we have substituted the emotional adjective "stagnant." We have trained them to think of the Future as a promised land which favoured heroes attain—not as something which everyone reaches at the rate of sixty minutes an hour, whatever he does, whoever he is,

Your affectionate uncle

Screwtape [1]

That describes precisely the strategy Satan is using with maximum effectiveness against the church today. Lewis exposed in those few words the essence of the problem I hope to address in this book. When he wrote that mythical letter from Uncle Screwtape in the 1940s, Lewis was correctly diagnosing an ailment that has practically crippled the contemporary church.

The villainous Screwtape hated "mere Christianity" and desperately wanted to adorn it with worldly ideas, fads, trendy add-ons, and whatever else he could sell gullible Christians. Why? Because he knew those things can only water down and weaken the purity of the faith. Pure Christianity needs no embellishment: "[Christ's] divine power has granted to us *everything* pertaining to life and godliness" (2 Pet. 1:3, emphasis added).

My last major polemic work, *The Gospel According to Jesus,* ended with a reference to 2 Peter 1:3. That book dealt with the gospel message and explored the question of what it means to believe in the Lord Jesus Christ.

The book struck an emotional chord, which was no surprise to me, but I confess I was startled by the *volume* of the clamor it generated. I am now working on two more books that will address the "lordship salvation" controversy further from a study of the apostles' writings.

This book, however, is not about that issue. Here I am concerned with the current erosion of confidence in the perfect sufficiency of our spiritual resources in Christ.

I anticipate that this book, too, will stir some controversy—though it shouldn't. As Christians, we find complete sufficiency in Christ and His provisions for our needs. There's no such thing as an incomplete or deficient Christian. Our Savior's divine power has granted to us *everything* pertaining to life and godliness. Human wisdom offers nothing to augment that. Every Christian receives all he or she needs at the moment of salvation. Each one must grow and mature, but no necessary resource is missing. There's no need to search for something more.

When Jesus completed His redemptive work on Calvary, He cried out triumphantly, "It is finished" (John 19:30). The saving work was fulfilled, completed. Nothing was omitted. And all who are recipients of that salvation are granted everything pertaining to life and godliness through the true knowledge of Christ (2 Pet. 1:3). In Him we have wisdom, righteousness, sanctification, and redemption (1 Cor. 1:30). His grace is sufficient for every situation (2 Cor. 12:9). We are blessed with every spiritual blessing in Him (Eph. 1:3). By one offering He has perfected us forever (Heb. 10:14). We are complete in Christ (Col. 2:10). What can anyone add to that?

So to possess the Lord Jesus Christ is to have every spiritual resource. All strength, wisdom, comfort, joy, peace, meaning, value, purpose, hope, and fulfillment in life now and forever is bound up in Him. Christianity is an all-sufficient relationship with an all-sufficient Christ. There's no reason anyone who believes God's Word should struggle with such a self-evident truth.

But a widespread lack of confidence in Christ's sufficiency is threatening the contemporary church. Too many Christians have tacitly acquiesced to the notion that our riches in Christ, including Scripture, prayer, the indwelling Holy Spirit, and all the other spiritual resources we find in Christ simply are not adequate to meet people's real needs. Entire churches are committed to programs built on the presupposition that the apostles' teaching, fellowship, the breaking of bread, and prayer (Acts 2:42) aren't a full enough agenda for the church as it prepares to enter the complex and sophisticated world of the twenty-first century.

Sadly, many Christians are not aware of the truth about our Lord's sufficiency. I hope they will be after reading this book. The church is in dire need of a renewed appreciation of what it means to be complete in Christ.

The failure of modern Christians to understand and appropriate the riches of Christ has opened the door to all kinds of aberrant influences. Bad doctrine, legalism, libertinism, humanism, and secularization—to name a few—are eroding the foundations of the Christian faith. Those satanic assaults are more subtle and therefore more dangerous than the liberalism that splintered the church at the start of this century—and they are succeeding with alarming effectiveness.

In the past two decades or so, for example, theology has become more and more humanistic. The focus has shifted from God to people and their problems, and counseling has replaced worship and evangelism as the main program of many churches. Most seminaries now put more energy into teaching ministerial students psychology than training them to preach. Evidently they believe therapists can accomplish more good in Christians' lives than preachers and teachers. That mindset has taken the church by storm. Evangelicalism is infatuated with psychotherapy. Emotional and psychological disorders supposedly requiring prolonged analysis have become almost fashionable. An hour listening to almost any call-in talk show on Christian radio will confirm that these things are so. Or visit your local Christian bookstore and note the proliferation of so-called "Christian" recovery books. Virtually everywhere you look in the evangelical subculture, you can find evidence that Christians are becoming more and more dependent on therapists, support groups and other similar groups.

This shift in the church's focus did not grow out of some new insight gained from Scripture. Rather, it has seeped into the church from the world. It is an attack at the most basic level, challenging Christians' confidence in the sufficiency of Christ.

"My grace is sufficient for you," the Lord said to the apostle Paul (2 Cor. 12:9). The average Christian in our culture cynically views that kind of counsel as simplistic, unsophisticated, and naive. Can you imagine one of today's professional radio counselors simply telling a hurting caller that God's grace is enough to meet the need? Contemporary opinion is more utilitarian, valuing physical comfort more than spiritual well-being, self-esteem above Christlikeness, and good feelings over holy living. Many Christians seeking a sense of fulfillment have turned away from the rich resources of God's all-sufficient grace and are engrossed instead in a fruitless search for contentment in hollow human teachings.

Another evidence that many are losing confidence in Christ's sufficiency is the church's increasing fascination with pragmatic methodology. Counseling is not the only program that has supplanted teaching, fellowship, communion, and prayer as the chief activities of church life. Many churches have de-emphasized preaching and worship in favor of entertainment, apparently believing they must lure converts by appealing to fleshly interests. As if Christ Himself were in some way inadequate, many church leaders now believe they must excite people's fancies in order to win them. Burlesque is evangelicalism's latest rage, as church after church adopts the new philosophy.

This is precisely the problem that plagued Israel throughout the Old Testament. Again and again the Israelites put their confidence in chariots and horses, alliances with Egypt, fleshly wisdom, material wealth, military might, and other human means—anything other than the sufficiency of their God. Refusing to rely solely on their ample spiritual resources brought them only failure and humiliation.

Yet the church today is behaving exactly like Old Testament Israel. Where will it end? Will biblical Christianity completely fade from the scene before the church enters its third millennium? "When the Son of Man comes, will He find faith on the earth?" (Luke 18:8).

The church is foundering in a slough of worldliness and self-indulgence. We desperately need a generation of leaders with the courage to confront the trend. We need godly men and women committed to the truth that in Christ we inherit spiritual resources sufficient for every need, every problem—everything that pertains to life and godliness.

1

Resurrecting an Old Heresy

God is able to make all grace abound to you, that always having all sufficiency in everything, you may have an abundance for every good deed.

2 Corinthians 9:8

A PASTOR I KNOW OF WAS CONDUCTING A SERIES of meetings in several churches in North and South Carolina. He was staying in the home of some close friends in Asheville and traveling each night to wherever he was speaking that evening.

One night he was scheduled to speak at a church in Greenville, South Carolina, which is several hours from Asheville. Because he didn't have a car, some friends from Greenville offered to transport him to and from the meeting. When they arrived to pick him up, he bid farewell to his hosts and told them he hoped to be back by midnight or soon afterward.

After ministering at the Greenville church, he stayed awhile to enjoy some fellowship and then rode back to Asheville. Approaching the house, he saw the porch light on and assumed his hosts would be prepared for his arrival because he had discussed the time of his return with them.

As he got out of the car, he sent his driver on his way, saying, "You must hurry. You have a long drive back. I'm sure they're prepared for me; I'll have no problem."

He felt the bitter cold of the winter night as he walked the long distance to the house. By the time he reached the porch, his nose and ears were already numb. He tapped gently on the door but no one answered. He tapped a little harder, and then even harder—but still no reply. Finally, concerned about the intense cold, he beat on the kitchen door and on a side window. But there was still no response.

Frustrated and becoming colder by the moment, he decided to walk to a neighboring house so he could call and awaken his hosts. On the way he realized that knocking on someone's door after midnight wasn't a safe thing to do, so he decided to find a public telephone. It was as dark as it was cold, and the pastor wasn't familiar with the area. Consequently he walked for several miles. At one point he slipped in the wet grass growing beside the road and slid down a bank into two feet of water. Soaked and nearly frozen, he crawled back up to the road and walked farther until he finally saw a blinking motel light. He awakened the manager, who was gracious enough to let him use the telephone.

The bedraggled pastor made the call and said to his sleepy host, "I hate to disturb you, but I couldn't get anyone in the house to wake up. I'm several miles down the road at the motel. Could you come get me?"

To which his host replied, "My dear friend, you have a key in your overcoat pocket. Don't you remember? I gave it to you before you left."

The pastor reached into his pocket. Sure enough, there was the key.

That true story illustrates the predicament of Christians who try to gain access to God's blessings through human means, all the while possessing Christ, who is the key to every spiritual blessing. He alone fulfills the deepest longings of our hearts and supplies every spiritual resource we need.

Believers have in Christ everything they will ever need to meet any trial, any craving, any difficulty they might ever encounter in this life. Even the newest convert possesses sufficient resources for every spiritual need. From the moment of salvation each believer is in Christ (2 Cor. 5:17) and Christ is in the believer (Col. 1:27). The Holy Spirit abides within as well (Rom. 8:9)—the Christian is His temple (1 Cor. 6:19). "Of His fulness we have all received, and grace upon grace" (John 1:16). So every Christian is a self-contained treasury of divinely bestowed spiritual affluence. There is nothing more—no great transcendental secret, no ecstatic experience, no hidden spiritual wisdom—that can take Christians to some higher plane of spiritual life. "His divine power has granted to us *everything* pertaining to life and godliness, through the true knowledge of Him who called us" (2 Pet. 1:3, emphasis added). "The true knowledge of *Him*" refers to a saving knowledge. To seek something more is like frantically knocking on a door, seeking what is inside, not realizing you hold the key in your pocket.

Satan has always tried to beguile Christians away from the purity and simplicity of an all-sufficient Christ (2 Cor. 11:3)—and he has always found people willing to forsake the truth for almost anything new and unusual.

Gnosticism's Invasion of the Early Church

One of the earliest denials of Christ's sufficiency was gnosticism, a cult that flourished in the first four centuries of church history. Many of the pseudo-biblical writings, including The Gospel of Thomas, The Gospel of Mary, The Apocryphon of John, The Wisdom of Jesus Christ, and The Gospel of Philip were gnostic works.

Gnostics believed matter is evil and spirit is good. They invented heretical explanations of how Christ could be God (pure, undefiled spirit), yet take on human flesh (which they viewed as a wholly evil material substance). Gnostics taught that there is a spark of divinity within human beings, and that the essence of spirituality is nurturing this immaterial side and denying material and physical urges. They believed that the chief means of releasing the divine element within a person was through attaining intellectual and spiritual enlightenment.

Gnostics therefore believed they were privy to a higher level of spiritual knowledge than the average believer had access to, and this secret realm of knowledge was the key to spiritual illumination. In fact, the Greek word *gnōsis* means "knowledge." The gnostic heresy caused many in the church to seek hidden knowledge beyond what God had revealed in His Word and through His Son.

Gnosticism was therefore a very elite, exclusive movement that disdained "unenlightened" and "simplistic" biblical Christians for their naiveté and lack of sophistication. Sadly, many in the church were beguiled by those ideas and drawn away from their confidence in Christ alone.

Gnosticism was an attack on the sufficiency of Christ. It held out the false promise of something more, some higher or more complete spiritual resource, when the truth is that Christ is all anyone could ever need.

Most of the New Testament epistles explicitly confront incipient forms of gnosticism. In Colossians, for example, the apostle Paul was attacking gnostic concepts when he wrote of "all the wealth that comes from the full assurance of understanding, resulting in a true knowledge of God's mystery, that is, Christ Himself, in whom are hidden all the treasures of wisdom and knowledge" (2:2–3). He warned believers against the emerging heresy's methodology: "See to it that no one takes you captive through philosophy and empty deception, according to the tradition of men, according to the elementary principles of the world, rather than according to Christ. For in Him all the fulness of Deity dwells in bodily form, and in Him you have been made complete, and He is the head over all rule and authority" (2:8–10; see further discussion in chapter 8).

Neo-Gnosticism's Attack on the Contemporary Church

Gnosticism never really died. Strains of gnostic influence have infected the church throughout history. Now a neo-gnostic tendency to seek hidden knowledge is gaining new influence with distressing results.

Where imprecise doctrine and careless biblical exegesis are tolerated, and where biblical wisdom and discernment languish, people always tend to look for something more than the simple sufficiency God has provided in Christ. Today as never before the church has grown careless and hazy with regard to biblical truth, and that has led to an unprecedented

29

quest for hidden knowledge. That is neo-gnosticism, and three major trends in the church today indicate it is gaining momentum: psychology, pragmatism, and mysticism.

Psychology. Nothing epitomizes neo-gnosticism more than the church's fascination with humanistic psychology. The integration of modern behavioral theory into the church has created an environment in which traditional counseling from the Bible is widely viewed as unsophisticated, naive, and even fatuous. The neo-gnostics would have us believe that sharing Scripture and praying with someone who is deeply hurting emotionally is too superficial. Only those who are trained in psychology—those with the secret knowledge—are qualified to help people with serious spiritual and emotional problems. The acceptance of that attitude is misleading millions and crippling church ministry.

The word *psychology* is a good one. Literally it means "the study of the soul." As such it originally carried a connotation that has distinctly Christian implications, for only someone who has been made complete in Christ is properly equipped to study the human soul. But pyschology cannot really study the soul; it is limited to studying human behavior. There is certainly value in that, but a clear distinction must be made between the contribution behavioral studies make to the educational, industrial, and physical needs of a society and their ability to meet the spiritual needs of people. Outside the Word and the Spirit there are no solutions to any of the problems of the human soul. Only God knows the soul and only God can change it. Yet the widely accepted ideas of modern psychology are theories originally developed by atheists on the assumption that there is no God and the individual alone has the power to change himself into a better person through certain techniques.

Surprisingly, the church has embraced many of the popular theories of secular psychology, and their impact over the past few years has been revolutionary. Many in the church believe the atheistic notion that people's "psychological problems" are distresses that are neither physical nor spiritual. "Christian psychologists" have become the new champions of church counseling. They are now heralded as the true healers of the human heart. Pastors and lay people are made to feel ill-equipped to counsel unless they have formal training in psychological techniques.

The clear message is that simply pointing Christians to their spiritual sufficiency in Christ is inane and maybe even dangerous. But on the contrary, it is inane and dangerous to believe that any problem is beyond the scope of Scripture or unmet by our spiritual riches in Christ.

Pragmatism. Does the end justify the means? Evangelicals like never before appear to be answering yes. Churches zealous to attract the unchurched have baptized virtually every form of amusement.

The early Christians met to worship, pray, fellowship, and be edified—and scattered to evangelize unbelievers. Many today believe instead that church meetings should entertain unbelievers for the purpose of creating a good experience that will make Christ more palatable to them. More and more churches are eliminating preaching from their worship services and opting instead for drama, variety shows, and the like. Some churches relegate Bible teaching to a midweek service; others have dropped it altogether. Those with access to the secret knowledge tell us that biblical preaching by itself cannot possibly be relevant. They say the church must adopt new methods and innovative programs to grab people on the level where they live.

That kind of pragmatism is quickly replacing super-naturalism in many churches. It is an attempt to achieve spiritual objectives by human methodology rather than supernatural power. Its primary criterion is external success. It will employ whatever method draws a crowd and stimulates the desired response. Its underlying presuppositions are that the church can accomplish spiritual goals by fleshly means, and that the power of God's Word alone is not sufficient to break through a sinner's blindness and hardness of heart.

I don't believe that is an overstatement. The wave of pragmatism sweeping the church today seems predicated on the idea that artificial technique and human strategy are *crucial* to the church's mission. Many appear to believe that we can capture people for Christ and the church only if our programs are imaginative enough and our sermons are persuasive enough. Therefore they bend their philosophy of ministry to suit whatever techniques seem to satisfy the most unbelievers.

Mysticism. Mysticism is the belief that spiritual reality is perceived apart from the human intellect and natural senses. It looks for truth internally, weighing feelings, intuition, and other internal sensations more heavily than objective, observable, external data. Mysticism ultimately derives its authority from a self-actualized, self-authenticated light rising from within. Its source of truth is spontaneous feeling rather than objective fact. The most extreme and complex forms of mysticism are found in Hinduism and its western reflection, New Age philosophy.

Thus an irrational and anti-intellectual mysticism that is the antithesis of Christian theology has infiltrated the church. In many cases individual feelings and personal experience have replaced sound biblical interpretation. The question "What does the Bible mean *to me*?" has become more important than "What does the Bible *mean*?"

That is a frightfully reckless approach to Scripture. It undermines biblical integrity and authority by implying that personal experience is to be sought more than an understanding of Scripture. It often considers private "revelations" and personal opinions equal to the eternal truth of God's inspired Word. Thus it fails to honor God and exalts man instead. Worst of all, it can—and usually does—lead to the deadly delusion that error is truth.

Extreme varieties of mysticism have flourished in recent decades, hawked by purveyors who make a platform of the religious broadcasting media. Televised religious talk shows have showcased almost every conceivable theological and interpretive whim by careless and untrained people—ranging from those who claim to have traveled to heaven and back, to those who deceive their listeners with new truth supposedly revealed privately to them by God. This kind of mysticism has spawned several aberrations, including the signs and wonders movement and a false gospel that promises health, wealth, and prosperity. It is simply one more evidence of the gnostic revival that is sweeping the church and undermining faith in the sufficiency of Christ.

Given the size of the contemporary church, the neo-gnosticism of today poses a more far-reaching threat than its first-century predecessor. Moreover, the leaders of the early church were united in their opposition to the gnostic heresy. Sadly, that is not true today.

What can be done? Paul confronted gnosticism by pointing to our sufficiency in Christ (Col. 2:10). That remains the answer even today.

We will look closely in the following chapters at each of these three gnostic influences. We will observe how they challenge Christ and His sufficiency, and we will discuss the spiritual resources available to all believers in Christ. As we proceed, you will note several repeated emphases: Scripture is sufficient, God's grace is sufficient, God's wisdom is sufficient, God Himself is sufficient, and so on. These overlapping sufficiencies show the incredible richness of the vast inheritance that is ours in our all-sufficient Christ.

2

Treasure or Trash?

We are children of God, and if children, heirs also, heirs of God and fellow heirs with Christ.

Romans 8:16–17

HOMER AND LANGLEY COLLYER WERE SONS OF a respected New York doctor. Both had earned college degrees. In fact, Homer had studied at Columbia University to become an attorney. When old Dr. Collyer died in the early part of this century, his sons inherited the family home and estate. The two men—both bachelors—were now financially secure.

But the Collyer brothers chose a peculiar lifestyle not at all consistent with the material status their inheritance gave them. They lived in almost total seclusion. They boarded up the windows of their house and padlocked the doors. All their utilities—including water—were shut off. No one was ever seen coming or going from the house. From the outside it appeared empty.

Though the Collyer family had been quite prominent, almost no one in New York society remembered Homer and Langley Collyer by the time World War II ended.

On March 21, 1947, police received an anonymous telephone tip that a man had died inside the boarded-up house. Unable to force their way in through the front door, they entered the house through a second-story window. Inside they found Homer Collyer's corpse on a bed. He had died clutching the February 22, 1920, issue of the *Jewish Morning Journal*, though he had been totally blind for years. This macabre scene was set against an equally grotesque backdrop.

It seems the brothers were collectors. They collected everything—especially junk. Their house was crammed full of broken machinery, auto parts, boxes, appliances, folding chairs, musical instruments, rags, assorted odds and ends, and bundles of old newspapers. Virtually all of it was worthless. An enormous mountain of debris blocked the front door; investigators were forced to continue using the upstairs window for weeks while excavators worked to clear a path to the door.

Nearly three weeks later, as workmen were still hauling heaps of refuse away, someone made a grisly discovery. Langley Collyer's body was buried beneath a pile of rubbish some six feet away from where Homer had died. Langley had been crushed to death in a crude booby trap he had built to protect his precious collection from intruders.

The garbage eventually removed from the Collyer house totaled more than 140 tons. No one ever learned why the brothers were stockpiling their pathetic treasure, except an old friend of the family recalled that Langley once said he was saving newspapers so Homer could catch up on his reading if he ever regained his sight.

Homer and Langley Collyer make a sad but fitting parable of the way many people in the church live. Although the Collyers' inheritance was sufficient for all their needs,

they lived their lives in unnecessary, self-imposed deprivation. Neglecting abundant resources that were rightfully
theirs to enjoy, Homer and Langley instead turned their
home into a squalid dump. Spurning their father's sumptu-
ous legacy, they binged instead on the scraps of the world.

A Rich Legacy to Enjoy

Too many Christians live their spiritual lives that way.
Disregarding the bountiful riches of an inheritance that
cannot be defiled (1 Pet. 1:4), they scour the wreckage of worldly
wisdom, collecting litter. As if the riches of God's grace (Eph.
1:7) were not enough, as if "everything pertaining to life and
godliness" (2 Pet. 1:3) were not sufficient, they try to supplement the resources that are theirs in Christ. They spend their
lives pointlessly accumulating sensational experiences, novel
teachings, clever gurus, or whatever else they can find to
add to their hoard of spiritual experiences. Practically all of it is
utterly worthless. Yet some people pack themselves so full
of these diversions that they can't find the door to the truth
that would set them free. They forfeit treasure for trash.

Where did Christians ever get the notion that they
needed anything other than Christ? Is He somehow inadequate? Is His gift of salvation somehow deficient? Certainly
not. We are children of God, joint heirs with Christ, and
therefore beneficiaries of a richer legacy than the human
mind could ever comprehend (Rom. 8:16–17). Christians
are rich beyond measure. All true Christians are heirs together with Christ Himself.

Scripture has much to say about the Christian's inheritance. It is, in fact, the central point of our New Covenant

relationship with Christ. The writer of Hebrews referred to Christ as "the mediator of a new covenant, in order that . . . those who have been called may receive the promise of the eternal inheritance" (Heb. 9:15).

We were chosen for adoption into God's own family before the world began (Eph. 1:4–5). With our adoption came all the rights and privileges of family membership, including an inheritance in time and eternity that is beyond our ability to exhaust.

This was a key element in the theology of the early church. In Acts 26:18 Paul says he was commissioned by Christ to preach to the Gentiles "so that they may turn from darkness to light and from the dominion of Satan to God, in order that they may receive forgiveness of sins and an inheritance among those who have been sanctified by faith in [Christ]." In Colossians 1:12 he says that God the Father has "qualified us to share in the inheritance of the saints in light." Paul viewed the believer's inheritance as so enormous in scope that he prayed the Ephesians would have the spiritual enlightenment to comprehend the richness of its glory (Eph. 1:18).

The concept of an inheritance from God had great significance to early Jewish believers in Christ because their Old Testament forefathers received the land of Canaan as an inheritance as part of God's covenant with Abraham (Gen. 12:1). Theirs was for the most part an earthly, material inheritance (Deut. 15:4; 19:10), though it included many spiritual blessings. Our inheritance in Christ, however, is primarily spiritual. That is, it is not a promise of wealth and material prosperity. It goes far beyond cheap temporal or transient physical blessings:

We Inherit God. This concept was a key to the Old Testament understanding of a spiritual inheritance. Joshua

13:33 says, "To the tribe of Levi, Moses did not give an [earthly] inheritance; the Lord, the God of Israel, is their inheritance, as He had promised to them." Of the twelve tribes of Israel, Levi had a uniquely spiritual function: it was the priestly tribe. As such its members did not inherit a portion of the Promised Land. The Lord Himself was their inheritance. They literally inherited God as their own possession.

David said, "The Lord is the portion of my inheritance" (Ps. 16:5). In Psalm 73:25–26 Asaph says, "Whom have I in heaven but Thee? / And besides Thee, I desire nothing on earth. / . . . God is the strength of my heart and my [inheritance] forever."

The prophet Jeremiah said, "The Lord is my portion . . . therefore I have hope in Him" (Lam. 3:24). That Old Testament principle applies to every Christian. We are "heirs of God" (Rom. 8:17). First Peter 2:9 describes believers as "a chosen race, a royal priesthood, a holy nation, a people for God's own possession." We are His and He is ours. What a joy to know that we inherit God Himself and will spend eternity in His presence!

We Inherit Christ. Believers enter into an eternal oneness with Christ. Christ Himself indwells them (Col. 1:27). He prayed to the Father "that they may be one, just as We are one; I in them, and Thou in Me" (John 17:22–23). Someday "we shall be like Him, because we shall see Him just as He is" (1 John 3:2) and we will reign with Him as joint heirs (Rom. 8:17).

We Inherit the Holy Spirit. Ephesians 1:14 says that the Holy Spirit "is given as a pledge of our inheritance." That is, He is the Guarantor of our inheritance. The Greek word translated "pledge" (*arrabōn*) originally referred to a down payment—money given to secure a purchase. It came to represent any token of a pledge. A form of the word even came to be used for an engagement ring. The Holy Spirit is the resident guarantee of our eternal inheritance.

We Inherit Salvation. Peter said our inheritance includes "a salvation ready to be revealed in the last time" (1 Pet. 1:5). The Greek word translated "salvation" speaks of a rescue or deliverance. In its broadest sense it refers to our full and final deliverance from the curse of the law; the power and presence of sin; and grief, pain, death, and judgment. No matter how difficult our present circumstances might be, we can look beyond them and bless God for the ultimate fullness of our eternal salvation.

We Inherit the Kingdom. Jesus said in Matthew 25:34: "The King will say to those on His right, 'Come, you who are blessed of My Father, inherit the kingdom prepared for you from the foundation of the world.'"

And so, we inherit God, Christ, the Holy Spirit, eternal salvation, and the kingdom. Still, the fullness of our inheritance has not yet been revealed to us. John wrote, "Dear friends, now we are children of God, and what we will be has not yet been made known" (1 John 3:2, NIV). Paul said, "No eye has seen, / no ear has heard, / no mind has conceived / what God has prepared for those who love him" (1 Cor. 2:9, NIV).

We're like a child prince who is too young and immature to understand the favored privileges of his position or the royal inheritance that awaits him. Consequently he may struggle with petty wants and throw tantrums over trinkets that pale in comparison to the riches he has access to and the ones he will receive when he assumes his father's throne. As he grows up, his parents must discipline and train him so he learns to behave like someone of royal lineage. Throughout that training and maturing process he begins to understand the unfolding value and implications of his inheritance.

We, too, will someday experience the fullness of our inheritance. In the meantime we must learn to act like children of the King, and let the hope of future blessings purify our lives (1 John 3:3).

Two Revolutionary Concepts

Focusing on our eternal inheritance is a key factor in maintaining a proper perspective on the sufficiency of Christ, especially in the middle of difficult circumstances. That's not always easy because we're prone toward selfishness and instant gratification. Advertising feeds that mentality by telling us we can have all we want—and we can have it *right now!* Of course "having it all" usually means buying on credit whatever product they're selling. A steady diet of that philosophy has fattened our society with self-indulgence and impatience. People find it difficult to cope with life if they can't instantly gratify every desire. They want to eliminate any discomfort, difficulty, injustice, or deprivation immediately.

Scripture responds with two revolutionary concepts: heavenly mindedness and delayed gratification. Heavenly mindedness is taking our eyes off the world's offerings for fulfillment and focusing them on God's sufficient provision for our satisfaction. It's what Jesus meant when He instructed us to make the Father's kingdom our first priority (Matt. 6:33). It's what Paul meant when he told us to set our minds on the things above, not on earthly things (Col. 3:2). And it's what John meant when he said, "Do not love the world, nor the things in the world" (1 John 2:15).

Delayed gratification is simply deferring to God's will and God's timing—the essence of patience. All His promises will be fulfilled, His righteousness and authority will be fully realized, His Son and His saints will be fully vindicated—but in His time, not ours. Many of the difficulties we experience will not be resolved in this life because His purposes transcend our temporal situations. So there's no point in running impatiently for relief to people offering "solutions" that ignore God's objectives and timetable.

For example, the Holy Spirit encourages persecuted believers to "be patient . . . until the coming of the Lord. Behold, the farmer waits for the precious produce of the soil, being patient about it, until it gets the early and late rains. You too be patient; strengthen your hearts, for the coming of the Lord is at hand" (James 5:7–8). I'm sure the dear saints to whom James was writing longed for God's comfort and justice against their persecutors; but God wanted them to cultivate patience, strength of heart, and a joyful anticipation of Christ's return. Those are far greater benefits than immediate relief from the difficulties and injustices they faced. God would vindicate them, but in His own time.

Adoring God for Our Eternal Inheritance

Heavenly minded patience includes looking forward to our eternal inheritance and adoring God for it despite our temporal circumstances. Peter illustrated that principle in his first epistle, which was written to teach us how to live out our faith amid seemingly unbearable trials and persecutions. The Emperor Nero had accused the Christians of burning

Rome, and the resulting persecution was spreading even as far as Asia Minor, where the recipients of 1 Peter lived.

To help them focus on their eternal inheritance rather than their present difficulties, Peter gave them—and us—a threefold word of encouragement.

Remember Your Calling. We are "a chosen race, a royal priesthood, a holy nation, a people for God's own possession" (1 Pet. 2:9). As such we are at odds with Satan's evil world system and will incur its wrath. Therefore we shouldn't be surprised or intimidated by threats of persecution. That's our calling:

> [We] have been called for this purpose, since Christ also suffered for [us], leaving [us] an example . . . to follow in His steps, who committed no sin, nor was any deceit found in His mouth; and while being re-viled, He did not revile in return; while suffering, He uttered no threats, but kept entrusting Himself to Him who judges righteously. (1 Pet. 2:21–23)

Remember to Praise God. Bowing in praise is far better than bowing to pressure. In 1 Peter 1:3–5 Peter says:

> Blessed be the God and Father of our Lord Jesus Christ, who according to His great mercy has caused us to be born again to a living hope through the res-urrection of Jesus Christ from the dead, to obtain an inheritance which is imperishable and undefiled and will not fade away, reserved in heaven for you, who are protected by the power of God through faith for a salvation ready to be revealed in the last time.

The main verb "be" (v. 3) is implied rather than stated ("Blessed *be* the God"). The text could be literally

45

translated, "Bless the God and Father of our Lord Jesus Christ." In short, the sense of it is "bless God," which is both a doxology and a command.

For Peter to have to command believers to bless God clearly illustrates the depth of our sinfulness. One of the joys of heaven will be our undiminished capacity to praise God perfectly and incessantly for His saving grace. The song of the redeemed will be on our lips throughout eternity. Yet now we struggle with apathy and familiarity. What an indictment! Praising God for our eternal inheritance should be the constant expression of our hearts, no matter what the temporal situation might be.

Remember Your Inheritance. Focusing on our inheritance is an important key to experiencing joy amid trials. The richness of our inheritance should motivate us to bless God continually. We're aliens in this world (1 Pet. 1:1), but we're citizens of heaven and recipients of immeasurable blessings in Christ.

How We Received Our Inheritance

The Greek word translated "inheritance" in 1 Peter 1:4 (*klēronomia*) speaks of possessions passed down from generation to generation. You don't earn or purchase them; you receive them simply because you're a family member. Peter describes in verse 3 the means by which believers gain membership in the family of God: "[He] caused us to be born again to a living hope through the resurrection of Jesus Christ from the dead." We receive our eternal inheritance by means of spiritual rebirth—the only solution to our sinful condition and alienation from God. Jesus made that very clear when He said to the Jewish leader Nicodemus, "Unless one is born again, he cannot see the kingdom of God" (John 3:3). John 1:12–13 underscores the same truth: "As many as received [Christ], to them He gave the right to become children of God, even to those who believe in His name, who were born not of blood, nor of the will of the flesh, nor of the will of man, but of God."

We were first born as sinful creatures, dead in trespasses and sins and indulging the desires of our flesh and mind. We were by nature children of wrath, separate from Christ, having no hope, and without God in the world (Eph. 2:1–3, 12). We were no more able to change our condition than we could alter the color of our skin, or than a leopard could change its spots (Jer. 13:23).

A person in that condition must be transformed by the power of the Holy Spirit. Through the new birth, the Spirit makes a new creation in Christ (2 Cor. 5:17), taking up residence in the believer and transforming that person's thinking and behavior. Perspectives and values change and the focus shifts from self to Christ.

God's Word is essential to the new birth. Peter said, "You have been born again not of seed which is perishable but imperishable, that is, through the living and abiding word of God. . . . This is the word which was preached to you" (1 Pet. 1:23, 25). The Holy Spirit works through the Word to activate faith, which results in the new birth (Rom. 10:17).

Faith means trusting in the Lord Jesus Christ alone for salvation. Many people want to add other requirements to the gospel, such as religious ceremony, some code of conduct, church membership, or whatever. All of those things are human works. Salvation cannot be earned by works but is a gift of God's grace (Rom. 3:21–26). That is,

God does not ask us to reform as a prerequisite to being saved; He justifies us freely, then works His transforming power to change us into the image of Christ (2 Cor. 3:18).

Before Nicodemus came to Jesus by night (John 3:2), he was undoubtedly like the other Jewish religious leaders of his day—living by an external code of religious conduct apart from true love for God (John 8:42). They thought they could be saved by their own good works. But Jesus shattered that illusion when He told Nicodemus, in effect, that he would have to assume the role of a spiritual infant by setting aside all his religious error and approaching salvation all over again on God's terms.

Jesus illustrated His point by referring to a familiar event in Israel's history. At one point during Israel's wilderness wanderings, God had sent fiery serpents among the people because they had spoken against God and Moses. Many had been bitten and were dying. When Moses interceded for the people, God instructed him to place a bronze serpent on a pole. Those who looked upon the bronze serpent were healed of their snakebites (Num. 21:5–9). That was the image Jesus called up in Nicodemus's mind: "As Moses lifted up the serpent in the wilderness, even so must the Son of Man be lifted up; that whoever believes may in Him have eternal life. For God so loved the world, that He gave His only begotten Son, that whoever believes in Him should not perish, but have eternal life" (John 3:14–16).

That bronze serpent was symbolic of the spiritual healing that comes to all who turn from sin and look to Jesus, who was lifted up on a cross. Nicodemus had been bitten by the serpent of self-righteous religious legalism. He needed to acknowledge his helplessness and look to Christ alone for salvation.

The new birth gives "a living hope" (1 Pet. 1:3). It is perpetually alive because it is grounded in the living God, who will fulfill all His promises (Titus 1:2), and because it transcends this temporal life. Paul said, "To me, to live is Christ, and to die is gain" (Phil. 1:21). Physical death simply ushers us into Christ's presence, where our hope is eternally realized. Believers need never fear the grave because Christ has conquered death and has given a living hope to all who love Him.

Also, our hope is living because it's based on the resurrection of Jesus Christ from the dead (1 Pet. 1:3). Jesus said, "Because I live, you shall live also" (John 14:19) and, "I am the resurrection and the life; he who believes in Me shall live even if he dies" (11:25). Then He raised Lazarus from the dead to prove His claim (vv. 43–44).

The Nature of Our Inheritance

Peter used three negative terms in 1 Peter 1:4 to describe the positive perfection of our inheritance: *imperishable, undefiled,* and *unfading.* The Greek word translated "imperishable" (*aphthartos*) speaks of something that is not corruptible, but permanent. The word evokes the image of a land ravaged by a conquering army. So Peter was saying our eternal inheritance cannot be plundered or spoiled by our spiritual foes.

"Undefiled" (*amiantos* in Greek) means unpolluted or unstained by sin, evil, or decay. Unlike this world, in which nothing escapes the stain of sin (Rom. 8:20–23), our inheritance can never be contaminated, defiled, or in any way corrupted. It is unblemished and unstained by the presence or effects of sin (Rev. 21:27).

"Will not fade away," or "unfading," comes from a Greek term used of flowers. In this context it suggests a supernatural beauty that time cannot diminish. Peter used the same word with reference to the unfading crown of glory that faithful elders will receive when the Chief Shepherd appears (1 Pet. 5:4).

Those three terms picture a heavenly inheritance that is impervious to death, sin, and the effects of time. Considering the corrupting, damning influence of sin on the world, it is wonderful to know our inheritance in Christ is timeless and will never diminish.

The Security of Our Inheritance

The believer's inheritance is "reserved in heaven for you, who are protected by the power of God through faith for a salvation ready to be revealed in the last time" (1 Pet. 1:4–5). We need never fear the loss of our inheritance, since it is under God's own watchful care.

Not only is God watching over our inheritance, but He also is doing so in the safest of all places: heaven. That's where "neither moth nor rust destroys, and where thieves do not break in or steal" (Matt. 6:20), and where "nothing unclean and no one who practices abomination and lying, shall ever [enter], but only those whose names are written in the Lamb's book of life" (Rev. 21:27). "Outside are the dogs and the sorcerers and the immoral persons and the murderers and the idolaters, and everyone who loves and practices lying" (Rev. 22:15). No one will ever invade or plunder heaven. Therefore our inheritance is eternally secure.

Many Christians are confident that God is able to guard their inheritance but doubt He can guard *them*. They fear they will somehow lose their salvation and forfeit God's promises. That's a popular view but it overlooks the fact that God protects more than our inheritance—He protects *us* as well! Peter said, "You . . . are protected by the power of God through faith for a salvation ready to be revealed in the last time" (1 Pet. 1:4–5).

The word translated "protected" is a military term that speaks of a guard. Peter used the present tense to indicate that we are continually under guard. Implied is the idea that we need ongoing protection because we're in a constant battle with Satan and his forces.

It is God's omnipotent, sovereign power that guards us and guarantees our final victory. God, the ultimate Judge, has justified us in Christ, made us heirs with Him, and has given us His Spirit to ensure that the good work He started in us will be perfected (Phil. 1:6). He is able to keep us from stumbling, and to make us "stand in the presence of His glory blameless with great joy" (Jude 24). Not even Satan himself can condemn us (Rom. 8:33), so rather than fearing the loss of our inheritance we should continually rejoice in God's great grace and mercy.

Another guarantee of our inheritance is our persevering faith. Peter said we are protected by God's power *through faith* (1 Pet. 1:5). Faith is God's gift to us; we don't generate it on our own (Eph. 2:8–9; Phil. 1:29). Faith is aroused by grace, upheld by grace, and energized by grace. Grace reaches into the soul of the believer, generating and maintaining faith. By God's grace alone we trust Christ, and by grace we continue to believe.

Our inheritance is a glorious thing. No earthly thing compares to it. But we can lose sight of it through worldly pursuits and the quest for instant gratification. Dear friends, don't collect this world's trash and neglect the treasure of our unspeakable riches in Christ.

No matter what your circumstances might be, consider your eternal inheritance. Meditate on it. Let it fill your heart with praise to the One who has extended such grace to you. Let it motivate you to live to His glory. Don't pursue the quick fix—some worldly solution to the passing problems of life. This world's trials aren't even worthy to be compared with our eternal glory. And always remember that you have Christ, who is all-sufficient in everything now and forever.

3

Does God Need a Psychiatrist?

Thy testimonies also are my delight;
They are my counselors.

Psalm 119:24

This also comes from the Lord of hosts,
Who has made His counsel wonderful and His
wisdom great.

Isaiah 28:29

IN 1980, GRACE COMMUNITY CHURCH WAS HIT with a lawsuit charging that the pastors on our staff were negligent because we tried to help a suicidal young member of our church by giving him biblical truth. It was the first clergy malpractice case ever heard in the American court system. The secular media had a field day as the case dragged on for years. Some nationally aired tabloid-type programs even alleged that our church had encouraged the young man to kill himself, teaching him that suicide was a sure way to heaven. Of course, that was not true. He knew from Scripture that suicide is wrong. We urged him to let the Word of God lead him to intimate knowledge and appropriation of the resources available in the One who wanted to heal his troubled mind. Tragically, he refused our counsel and took his own life.

One of the key issues the case raised was the question of whether churches should have the legal right to counsel troubled people with the Bible. Many would argue that giving someone advice from Scripture is a simplistic approach to counseling. The Bible may be fine as an encouragement to the average person, we are told, but people who have *real* problems need a psychological expert's help.

Therefore, this lawsuit contended, church counselors are obligated to refer seriously depressed and suicidal people to mental-health professionals. To attempt to counsel these troubled people from the Bible amounts to irresponsibility and negligence for which church counselors should be held morally and legally culpable.

The truth that came out in court received little or no coverage on the network news. Testimony showed that this young man *was* under the care of professional psychiatrists. In addition to the biblical direction he received from our pastoral staff, he *had* sought psychiatric treatment. Moreover, our staff had seen to it that he was examined by several medical doctors, to rule out organic or chemical causes for his depression. He was receiving every kind of therapy available, but he chose to end his life anyway. We did all we could to help him; he rejected our counsel and turned his back on his spiritual sufficiency in Christ.

Not only did the courts view the issue as a First Amendment right of religious freedom into which government should not intrude, but all three times we won the case, the judges also expressed the opinion that the church had *not* failed in its responsibility to give him proper care. Their judgment was that our staff had more than fulfilled their legal and moral obligations by trying to help this young man who had sought our counsel. Eventually the case was appealed even to the United States Supreme Court. The High Court refused to hear the case, thereby letting stand the California State Supreme Court's ruling, which vindicated the church. Most important of all, the case affirmed every church's constitutional right to counsel from the Bible, establishing a legal precedent to keep secular courts from encroaching on the area of counseling in the church.

The Professionalization of the Counseling Ministry

Unfortunately, the privilege of counseling people with biblical truth may be in jeopardy anyway—not because of any legal barrier imposed from outside the church, but because of the attitude toward Scripture within the church. During the trial, a number of "experts" were called to give testimony. Most surprising to me were the so-called Christian psychologists and psychiatrists who testified that the Bible alone does not contain sufficient help to meet people's deepest personal and emotional needs. These men were actually arguing before a secular court that God's Word is not an adequate resource for counseling people about their spiritual problems! What is truly appalling is the number of evangelicals who are willing to take such "professionals'" word for it.

Over the past decade a host of evangelical psychological clinics have sprung up. Though almost all of them claim to offer biblical counsel, most merely dispense secular psychology disguised in spiritual terminology. Moreover, they are removing the counseling ministry from its proper arena in the church body and conditioning Christians to think of themselves as incompetent to counsel. Many pastors, feeling inadequate and perhaps afraid of possible malpractice litigation, are perfectly willing to let "professionals" take over what used to be seen as a vital pastoral responsibility.

Too many have bought the lie that a crucial realm of wisdom exists outside Scripture and one's relationship to Jesus Christ, and that some idea or technique from that extrabiblical realm holds the real key to helping people with their deep problems.

True psychology ("the study of the soul") can be done only by Christians, since only Christians have the resources for the understanding and the transformation of the soul. Since the secular discipline of psychology is based on godless assumptions and evolutionary foundations, it is capable of dealing with people only superficially and only on the temporal level. The Puritans, long before the arrival of godless psychology, identified their ministry with people as "soul work."

Scripture is the manual for all "soul work" and is so comprehensive in the diagnosis and treatment of every spiritual matter that, energized by the Holy Spirit in the believer, it leads to making one like Jesus Christ. This is the process of biblical sanctification.

It is reasonable for people to seek medical help for a broken leg, dysfunctional kidney, tooth cavity, or other physical malady. It is also sensible for someone who is alcoholic, drug addicted, learning disabled, traumatized by rape, incest, or severe battering to seek some help in trying to cope with their trauma.

Certain techniques of human psychology can serve to lessen trauma or dependency and modify behavior in Christians or non-Christians equally. There may also be certain types of emotional illnesses where root causes are organic and where medication might be needed to stabilize an otherwise dangerous person. These are relatively rare problems, however, and should not be used as examples to justify this indiscriminate use of secular psychological techniques for essentially spiritual problems. Dealing with the physical and emotional issues of life in such ways is *not* sanctification!

"Christian psychology" as the term is used today is an oxymoron. The word *psychology* no longer speaks of studying the soul; instead it describes a diverse menagerie of therapies and theories that are fundamentally humanistic. The presuppositions and most of the doctrine of psychology cannot be successfully integrated with Christian truth. Moreover, the infusion of psychology into the teaching of the church has blurred the line between behavior modification and sanctification.

The path to wholeness is the path of spiritual sanctification. Would we foolishly turn our backs on the Wonderful Counselor, the spring of living water, for the sensual wisdom of earth and the stagnant water of behaviorism?

Our Lord Jesus reacted in a perfect and holy way to every temptation, trial, and trauma in life—and they were more severe than any human could ever suffer. Therefore, it should be clear that perfect victory over all life's troubles must be the result of being like Christ.

No "soul worker" can lift another above the level of spiritual maturity he is on. So the supreme qualification for psychologists would be Christlikeness.

If one is a truly Christian psychologist, he must be doing soul work in the realm of the deep things of the Word and the Spirit—not fooling around in the shallows of behavior modification. Why should a believer choose to do behavior modification when he has the tools for spiritual transformation (like a surgeon wreaking havoc with a butter knife instead of using a scalpel)? The most skilled counselor is the one who most carefully, prayerfully, and faithfully applies the divine sanctification—shaping another into the image of Jesus Christ.

There may be no more serious threat to the life of the church today than the stampede to embrace the doctrines of secular psychology. They are a mass of human ideas that Satan has placed in the church as if they were powerful, life-changing truths from God. Most psychologists epitomize neo-gnosticism, claiming to have secret knowlege for solving people's real problems. There are even those psychologists who claim to perform a therapeutic technique they call "Christian counseling" but in reality are using secular theory to treat spiritual problems with biblical references tacked on.

The result is that pastors, biblical scholars, teachers of Scripture, and caring believers using the Word of God are disdained as naive, simplistic, and altogether inadequate counselors. Bible reading and prayer are commonly belittled as "pat answers," incomplete solutions for someone struggling with depression or anxiety. Scripture, the Holy Spirit, Christ, prayer, and grace—those are the traditional solutions Christian counselors have pointed people to. But the average Christian today has come to believe that none of them *really* offers the cure for people's woes.

How Scientific Are the Behavioral Sciences?

Psychology is not a uniform body of scientific knowledge, like thermodynamics or organic chemistry. When we speak of psychology we refer to a complex menagerie of ideas and theories, many of which are contradictory. Psychology has not even proved capable of dealing effectively with the human mind and with mental and emotional processes. Thus it can hardly be regarded as a science.

Many, I'm sure, will object to my classifying psychology as a pseudo-science. But that's exactly what it is— the most recent of several human inventions designed to explain, diagnose, and treat behavioral problems without dealing with moral and spiritual issues. Little more than a century ago debate was raging over a different kind of "behavioral science" called phrenology. Phrenology held that personality characteristics were determined by the shape of someone's skull. You've probably seen old phrenologists' diagrams; they were maps of the head with specific areas labeled, showing which zone of the brain determined a particular emotion or characteristic. A phrenologist would feel people's skulls, diagnosing their problems by the location of bumps on their head.

If you think behavioral science has advanced greatly since then, ask yourself how reasonable it is to surround an adult in the fetal position with pillows so he can get back in touch with his prenatal anxieties. Given the choice, I believe I would opt for someone poking around on my head!

Modern psychologists use hundreds of counseling models and techniques based on a myriad of conflicting theories, so it is impossible to speak of psychotherapy as if it were a unified and consistent science. However, the following views, popularized by psychology, have filtered down into the church from the assorted stuff in the psychological tank and are having a profound and disturbing effect on its approach to helping people:

- Human nature is basically good.
- People have the answers to their problems inside them.

- The key to understanding and correcting a person's attitudes and actions lies somewhere in his past.
- Individuals' problems are the result of what someone else has done to them.
- Human problems can be purely psychological in nature—unrelated to any spiritual or physical condition.
- Deep-seated problems can be solved only by professional counselors using therapy.
- Scripture, prayer, and the Holy Spirit are inadequate and simplistic resources for solving certain types of problems.

Ironically, even before the church became so infatuated with "behavioral science," those who know it best were beginning to question whether psychotherapy is a science at all. Eleven years ago, *Time* magazine ran a cover story called "Psychiatry on the Couch." It said this:

> On every front, psychiatry seems to be on the defensive. . . . Many psychiatrists want to abandon treatment of ordinary, everyday neurotics ("the worried well") to psychologists and the amateur Pop therapists. After all, does it take a hard-won M.D. degree . . . to chat sympathetically and tell a patient you're-much-too-hard-on-yourself? And if psychiatry is a medical treatment, why can its practitioners not provide measurable scientific results like those obtained by other doctors?
>
> Psychiatrists themselves acknowledge that their profession often smacks of modern alchemy—full of jargon, obfuscation and mystification, but precious little real knowledge. . . .

As always, psychiatrists are their own severest critics. Thomas Szasz, long the most outspoken gadfly of his profession, insists that there is really no such thing as mental illness, only normal problems of living. E. Fuller Torrey, another antipsychiatry psychiatrist, is willing to concede that there are a few brain diseases, like schizophrenia, but says they can be treated with only a handful of drugs that could be administered by general practitioners or internists. . . . By contrast, the Scottish psychiatrist and poet R. D. Laing is sure that schizophrenia is real—and that it is good for you. Explains Laing: it is a kind of psychedelic epiphany, far superior to normal experience.

Even mainline practitioners are uncertain that psychiatry can tell the insane from the sane.[1]

The article went on to chronicle the failures of psychiatry, noting that "of all patients, one-third are eventually 'cured,' one-third are helped somewhat, and one-third are not helped at all."[2] But as the article further stated,

The trouble is that most therapies, including some outlandish ones, also claim some improvement for two-thirds of their patients. Critics argue that many patients go into analysis after a traumatic experience, such as divorce or a loved one's death, and are bound to do better anyway when the shock wears off. One study shows improvement for people merely on a waiting list for psychoanalytic treatment; presumably the simple decision to seek treatment is helpful.[3]

The article concludes with a pessimistic forecast by Ross Baldessarini, a psychiatrist and biochemist at the Mailman Research Center. He told *Time*, "We are not going to find the causes and cures of mental illness in the foreseeable future."[4]

Several years later, a conference in Phoenix, Arizona, brought together the world's leading experts on psychotherapy for what was billed as the largest meeting ever held on the subject. The conference, called "The Evolution of Psychotherapy," drew 7,000 mental-health experts from all over the world. It was the largest such gathering in history, billed by its organizer as the Woodstock of psychotherapy. Out of it came several stunning revelations.

The *Los Angeles Times*, for example, quoted Laing, who "said that he couldn't think of any fundamental insight into human relations that has resulted from a century of psychotherapy. 'I don't think we've gone beyond Socrates, Shakespeare, Tolstoy, or even Flaubert by the age of 15,'" he said.[5] Laing added,

> "I don't think psychiatry is a science at all. It's not like chemistry or physics where we build up a body of knowledge and progress."
> He said that in his current personal struggle with depression, humming a favorite tune to himself (he favors one called "Keep Right On to the End of the Road") sometimes is of greater help than anything psychotherapy offers.[6]

Time magazine, reporting on the conference, noted that in a panel discussion on schizophrenia, three out of four "experts" said there is no such disease.[7]

> R. D. Laing, the favorite shrink of student rebels in the '60s, retains his romantic opinion of schizophrenics as brave victims who are defying a cruel culture. He

suggested that many people are diagnosed as schizo-
phrenic simply because they sleep during the day and
stay awake at night. Schizophrenia did not exist until
the word was invented, he said. . . . At a later panel, a
woman in the audience asked Laing how he would deal
with schizophrenics. Laing bobbed and weaved for 27
minutes and finally offered the only treatment possible
for people he does not view as sick: "I treat them exactly the same way I treat anybody else. I conduct myself by the ordinary rules of courtesy and politeness."[8]

One truth came out clearly in the conference: among
therapists there is little agreement. There is no unified "science" of psychotherapy; only a cacophony of clashing theories and therapies. Dr. Joseph Wolpe, a leading pioneer of
behavioral therapy, characterized the Phoenix conference as
"a babel of conflicting voices."[9]

And indeed it was. One specialist, Jay Haley, described what he called his "shaggy dog" technique. Evidently
he means it is like a fluffy animal that appears to be fat until
it gets wet—there seems to be more substance than really
exists. This is his approach to therapy:

Get the patient to make an absolute commitment to
change, then guarantee a cure but do not tell the patient what it is for several weeks. "Once you postpone,
you never lose them as patients," he said. "They have to
find out what the cure is." One bulimic who ate in binges
and threw up five to 25 times a day was told she would
be cured if she gave the therapist a penny the first time
she vomited and doubled the sum each time she threw
up. Says Haley: "They quickly figure out that it doubles
so fast that they can owe the therapist hundreds of
thousands of dollars in a few days, so they stop."[10]

Jeffrey Zeig, organizer of the conference, said there may be as many as a hundred different theories in the United States alone. Most of them, he said, are "doomed to fizzle."[11]

Not only do psychologists sell supposed cures for a high price, but they also invent diseases for which the cures are needed. Their marketing strategy has been effective. Invent problems or difficulties, harp on them until people think they are hopelessly afflicted, then peddle a remedy. Some of the supposed problems of our culture are pathetically trite. Self-image, looks, co-dependency, emotional abuse, mid-life crisis, unfulfilled expectations—today's "infirmities" were once seen more accurately as the pains of selfishness. Egocentricity has become a major marketing strategy for psychotherapists. By fostering people's natural tendency toward self-indulgence, psychology has sold itself to an eager public. And the church has witlessly jumped on the bandwagon.

Psychology is no more a science than the atheistic evolutionary theory upon which it is based. Like theistic evolution, "Christian psychology" is an attempt to harmonize two inherently contradictory systems of thought. Modern psychology and the Bible cannot be blended without serious compromise to or utter abandonment of the principle of Scripture's sufficiency.

Though it has become a lucrative business, psychotherapy cannot solve anyone's spiritual problems. At best it can occasionally use human insight to superficially modify behavior. It succeeds or fails for Christians and non-Christians equally because it is only a temporal adjustment—a sort of mental chiropractic. It cannot change the human heart, and even the experts admit that.

The Failure of "Christian Psychology"

Meanwhile, however, the attitude within the church is more accepting of psychotherapy than ever. If the Christian media serve as a barometer of the whole church, a dramatic shift is taking place. Christian radio, for example, once a bastion of Bible teaching and Christian music, is overrun with talk shows, pop psychology, and phone-in psychotherapy. Preaching the Bible is passé. Psychologists and radio counselors are the new heroes of evangelicalism. And Christian radio is the major advertising tool for the selling of psychology—which is pulling in money by the billions.

The church is thereby ingesting heavy doses of dogma from psychology, adopting secular "wisdom" and attempting to sanctify it by calling it Christian. Evangelicalism's most fundamental values are thus being redefined. "Mental and emotional health" is the new buzzword. It is not a biblical concept, though many seem to equate it with spiritual wholeness. Sin is called sickness, so people think it requires therapy, not repentance. Habitual sin is called addictive or compulsive behavior, and many surmise its solution is medical care rather than moral correction.

Human therapies are embraced most eagerly by the spiritually weak—those who are shallow or ignorant of biblical truth and who are unwilling to accept the path of suffering that leads to spiritual maturity and deeper communion with God. The unfortunate effect is that these people remain immature, held back by a self-imposed dependence on some pseudo-Christian method or psycho-quackery that actually stifles real growth.

The more secular psychology influences the church, the further people move from a biblical perspective on problems and solutions. One-on-one therapists are replacing the Word, God's chief means of grace (1 Cor. 1:21; Heb. 4:12). The counsel these professionals dispense is often spiritually disastrous. Not long ago I listened aghast as a Christian psychologist on live radio counseled a caller to express anger at his therapist by making an obscene gesture at him. "Go ahead!" he told the caller. "It's an honest expression of your feelings. Don't try to keep your anger inside."

"What about my friends?" the caller asked. "Should I react that way to all of them when I'm angry?"

"Why, sure!" this counselor said. "You can do it to anyone, whenever you feel like it. Except those who you think won't understand—they won't be good therapists for you." That's a paraphrase. I have a tape of the entire broadcast, and what the counselor actually suggested was much more explicit, even to the point of being inappropriate to print.

That same week, I heard another popular Christian broadcast that offers live counseling to callers nationwide. A woman called and said she has had a problem with compulsive fornication for years. She said she goes to bed with "anyone and everyone" and feels powerless to change her behavior.

The counselor suggested that her conduct is her way of striking back, a result of wounds inflicted by her passive father and overbearing mother. "There's no simple road to recovery," this radio therapist told her. "Your problem won't go away immediately—it's an addiction, and these things require extended counseling. You will need years of therapy to overcome your need for illicit sex." The suggestion was then made for the caller to find a church that would be tolerant while she worked her way out of the "painful wounds" that were "making" her fornicate.

What kind of advice is that? First, the counselor in effect gave that woman permission to defer obedience to a clear command of Scripture: "Flee immorality" (1 Cor. 6:18; see also 1 Thess. 4:3). Second, he blamed her parents and justified her vengeance toward them. Third, he seemed to be suggesting she could taper off gradually from her sin— under therapy, of course.

Furthermore, he gave his nationwide audience the clear message that he has no real confidence in the Holy Spirit's power to immediately transform a person's heart and behavior. Worse, he encouraged churches to tolerate a person's sexual sin until therapy begins to work.

Contrast both of those radio counselors' advice with the profound simplicity of Galatians 5:16: "Walk by the Spirit, and you will not carry out the desire of the flesh." Do we really think years of therapy can bring people to the point where they walk by the Spirit? Certainly not if the therapist is someone who recommends obscene gestures, delayed repentance, and churches tolerant of chronic immorality! There is no biblical justification for such counsel—in fact, it flatly contradicts God's Word. The apostle Paul told the Corinthian church to turn an adulterer over to Satan, putting him out of the church (1 Cor. 5:1–13).

I thank God for men and women in the church who depend on the Bible when counseling others. I am grateful for godly counselors who urge troubled people to pray and who point them to Scripture, to God, and to the fullness of His resources for every need.

I have no quarrel with those who use either common sense or social sciences as a helpful observer's platform to look on human conduct and develop tools to assist people in getting some external controls in their behavior. That may be useful as a first step for getting to the real spiritual cure. But a wise counselor realizes that all behavioral therapy stops on the surface—far short of actual solutions to the real needs of the soul, which are resolved only in Christ.

On the other hand, I have no tolerance for those who exalt psychology above Scripture, intercession, and the perfect sufficiency of our God. And I have no encouragement for people who wish to mix psychology with the divine resources and sell the mixture as a spiritual elixir. Their methodology amounts to a tacit admission that what God has given us in Christ is not really adequate to meet our deepest needs and salve our troubled lives.

God Himself doesn't think very highly of counselors who claim to represent Him but rely instead on human wisdom. Job 12:17–20 says:

> He makes counselors walk barefoot [a sign of
>   humiliation],
> And makes fools of judges.
> He loosens the bond of kings,
> And binds their loins with a girdle.
> He makes priests walk barefoot,
> And overthrows the secure ones.
> He deprives the trusted ones of speech,
> And takes away the discernment of the elders.

God's wisdom is so vastly superior to man's that the greatest human counselors are made into a spectacle. Verses 24–25 add,

He deprives of intelligence the chiefs of the earth's
   people,
And makes them wander in a pathless waste.
They grope in darkness with no light,
And He makes them stagger like a drunken man.

If anyone had to endure the folly of well-intentioned
human counselors it was Job. Their irrelevant, useless advice was as much a grief to him as the satanic afflictions he
suffered.

The depth to which sanctified psychotherapy can sink
is really quite profound. A local newspaper recently featured
an article about a thirty-four-bed clinic that has opened up
in Southern California to treat "Christian sex addicts."[12] (The
reason for beds in this kind of clinic escapes me.) According
to the article, the clinic is affiliated with a large and well-
known Protestant church in the area. Its staff comprises
specialists described as "real pioneers in the area [of sexual
addictions]. These are all legitimate, licensed psychotherapists who happen to have a strong Christian orientation to
therapy," according to the center's director.[13]

Does their "Christian" orientation happen to be solid
enough to allow these psychotherapists to admit that las-
civiousness is sin? Evidently not. Several were interviewed
for the article. They consistently used the terms *illness,
problem, conflict,* and *compulsive behavior, treatment,* and
therapy. Words with moral overtones were carefully avoided.
Sin and repentance were never mentioned.

Worse, these so-called experts scoffed at the power
of God's Word to transform a heart and break the bondage of sexual sin. The article quoted the center's program

director, who explained why he believes his treatment center specifically for Christians is so crucial: "There are some groups of Christians who believe the Bible is all you need."[14]

That statement is the echo of neo-gnosticism. Belittling those who believe the Bible is sufficient, these latter-day "clouds without water" (Jude 12) insist they are privy to a higher, more sophisticated secret knowledge that holds the real answer to what troubles the human soul. Don't be intimidated by their false claims. No higher knowledge, no hidden truth, nothing besides the all-sufficient resources that we find in Christ exists that can change the human heart.

Any counselor who desires to honor God and be effective must see the goal of his efforts as leading a person to the sufficiency of Christ. The view that man is capable of solving his own problems, or that people can help one another by "therapy" or other human means, denies the doctrine of human depravity and man's need for God. It replaces the Spirit's transforming power with impotent human wisdom.

4

Truth in a
World of
Theory

Sanctify them in the truth; Thy word is truth.

John 17:17

IT IS SIGNIFICANT THAT ONE OF THE BIBLICAL names of Christ is Wonderful Counselor (Isa. 9:6). He is the highest and ultimate One to whom we may turn for counsel, and His Word is the well from which we may draw divine wisdom. What could be more wonderful than that? In fact, one of the most glorious aspects of Christ's perfect sufficiency is the wonderful counsel and great wisdom He supplies in our times of despair, confusion, fear, anxiety, and sorrow. He is the quintessential Counselor.

Now that is not to denigrate the importance of Christians counseling each other. There certainly is a crucial need for biblically sound counseling ministries within the body of Christ. I would not for a moment dispute the important role of those who are spiritually gifted to offer encouragement, discernment, comfort, advice, compassion, and help to others. In fact, one of the very problems that has led to the current plague of bad counsel is that churches have not done as well as they could in enabling people with those kinds of spiritual gifts to minister excellently. The complexities of this modern age make it more difficult than ever to take the time necessary to listen well, serve others through compassionate personal involvement, and otherwise provide the close fellowship necessary for the church body to enjoy health and vitality.

Churches have looked to psychology to fill the gap, but it isn't going to work. Professional psychologists are no substitute for spiritually gifted people, and the counsel psychology offers cannot replace biblical wisdom and divine power. Moreover, psychology tends to make people dependent on a therapist, whereas those exercising true spiritual gifts always turn people back to an all-sufficient Savior and His all-sufficient Word.

A Psalm on the Sufficiency of God's Word

King David was an example of someone who occasionally sought advice from human counselors, but always ultimately turned to God for answers. As many of the psalms reveal, he was especially dependent on God alone when he struggled with personal problems or emotions. When hit with depression or inner turmoil, he turned to God and wrestled in prayer. When the problem was his own sin, he was repentant, broken, and contrite. He prayed, "Examine me, O Lord, and try me; / Test my mind and my heart" (Ps. 26:2). The spiritually mature always turn to God for help in times of anxiety, distress, confusion, or unrest in the soul, and they are assured of wise counsel and deliverance.

That's because every need of the human soul is ultimately spiritual. There is no such thing as a "psychological problem" unrelated to spiritual or physical causes. God supplies divine resources sufficient to meet all those needs completely. David understood that. His writings reflect the depth of human experience, emotion, and spiritual insight of one who had fully experienced the extremities of life. He knew the exhilaration of going from shepherd to king. He wrote of everything from absolute triumph to bitter discouragement. He wrestled with pain so deep he could hardly bear to live. His own son Absalom tried to kill him and was then killed. He suffered from horrible guilt because of immorality and murder. His children brought him constant grief. He struggled to understand both the nature of God and his own heart. Of God he said, "Great is the Lord" (Ps. 145:3), while of himself he said, "Wash me thoroughly from my iniquity, / And cleanse me from my sin" (Ps. 51:2). He told God what he felt and cried out for relief—though he admitted God had every right to punish him.

At the end of some of David's psalms he looked out a window of hope, and sometimes he didn't. But David always went to God because he understood God's sovereignty and his own depravity. He knew that his all-sufficient Savior alone had the answers to his needs and the power to apply those answers. And he knew that those answers were to be found in the truth about God revealed in His Word, which is itself perfectly sufficient. The sufficient God revealed Himself in His sufficient Word.

Psalm 19:7–14 is the most monumental statement on the sufficiency of Scripture ever made in concise terms. Penned by David under the inspiration of the Holy Spirit, it offers an unwavering testimony from God Himself about the sufficiency of His Word for every situation. It counters the teaching of those who believe we must augment God's Word with truth gleaned from modern psychology:

> The law of the Lord is perfect, restoring the soul;
> The testimony of the Lord is sure, making wise the simple.
> The precepts of the Lord are right, rejoicing the heart;
> The commandment of the Lord is pure, enlightening the eyes.
> The fear of the Lord is clean, enduring forever;
> The judgments of the Lord are true; they are righteous altogether.
> They are more desirable than gold, yes, than much fine gold;
> Sweeter also than honey and the drippings of the honeycomb.
> Moreover, by them Thy servant is warned;
> In keeping them there is great reward.
> Who can discern his errors? Acquit me of hidden faults.
> Also keep back Thy servant from presumptuous sins;
> Let them not rule over me;
> Then I shall be blameless,
> And I shall be acquitted of great transgression.
> Let the words of my mouth and the meditation of my heart
> Be acceptable in Thy sight,
> O Lord, my rock and my Redeemer.

With an economy of words the Holy Spirit gives us a comprehensive catalog of the characteristics and benefits of Scripture, each of which merits our close investigation.

In verses 7–9 David makes six statements about Scripture. Each title for Scripture includes the phrase "of the Lord." In revealing the many-faceted general purpose of God's Word, he calls Scripture "the law of the Lord," "the testimony of the Lord," "the precepts of the Lord," "the commandment of the Lord," "the fear of the Lord," and "the judgments of the Lord." In each case "Lord" translates the Hebrew word *Yahweh*, which is the covenant name of God. Clearly David wanted us to know that Scripture proceeds from God Himself.

Each of the six statements highlights a characteristic of God's Word and describes its effect in the life of one who embraces it.

Scripture Is Perfect, Restoring the Soul. In the first statement (v. 7), he says, "The law of the Lord is perfect, restoring the soul." The Hebrew word translated "law" is *torah*, which emphasizes the didactic nature of Scripture. Here David uses it to refer to Scripture as the sum of what God has revealed for our instruction, whether it be creed (what we believe), character (what we are), or conduct (what we do).

"Perfect" is the translation of a common Hebrew word meaning "whole," "complete," or "sufficient." It conveys the idea of something that is comprehensive, so as to cover all aspects of an issue. Commentator Albert Barnes wrote,

> The meaning [of "perfect"] is that [Scripture] lacks nothing [for] its completeness; nothing in order that it might be what it should be. It is complete as a revelation of Divine truth; it is complete as a rule of conduct. . . . It is absolutely true; it is adapted with consummate wisdom to the [needs] of man; it is an unerring guide of conduct. There is nothing there which would lead men into error or sin; there is nothing essential for man to know which may not be found there.[1]

Scripture is comprehensive, embodying all that is necessary to one's spiritual life. David's implied contrast is with the imperfect, insufficient, flawed reasoning of men.

God's perfect law, David said, affects people by "restoring the soul" (v. 7). The Hebrew word translated "restoring" can mean "converting," "reviving," or "refreshing," but my favorite synonym is "transforming." The word "soul" (in Hebrew, *nephesh*) refers to one's person, self, or heart. It is translated all those ways (and many more) in the Old Testament. The essence of it is the inner person, the whole person, the real you. To paraphrase David's words, Scripture is so powerful and comprehensive that it can convert or transform the entire person, changing someone into precisely the person God wants him to be. God's Word is sufficient to restore through salvation even the most broken life—a fact to which David himself gave abundant testimony.

Scripture Is Trustworthy, Imparting Wisdom. David, further expanding the sweep of scriptural sufficiency, writes in Psalm 19:7, "The testimony of the Lord is sure, making wise the simple." "Testimony" speaks of Scripture as a divine witness. Scripture is God's sure testimony to who He is and what He requires of us. "Sure" means His testimony is unwavering, immovable, unmistakable, reliable, and worthy to be trusted. It provides a foundation on which to build our lives and eternal destinies.

In 2 Peter 1:16–18 Peter reflects back to his time on the Mount of Transfiguration with all the supernatural events of that marvelous occasion (the majestic glory of Christ, the voice from heaven, and the appearance of Moses and Elijah). But despite all he had experienced, he says in verse 19, "We have more sure—the prophetic word" (literal translation).

In that statement Peter affirmed that the testimony of God's written Word is a surer and more convincing confirmation of God's truth than what he had personally seen and heard at the transfiguration of Christ. Unlike many today who cite spurious mystical experiences, Peter had a verifiable real-life encounter with Christ in His full glory on the mount. And in contrast with those today who advocate miracles as the necessary proof of God's power and presence, Peter looked to Scripture as a higher and more trustworthy authority than even such a dramatic experience. Commentator Samuel Cox has written,

> Peter knew a sounder basis for faith than that of signs and wonders. He had seen our Lord Jesus Christ receive honor and glory from God the Father in the holy mount; he had been dazzled and carried out of himself by visions and voices from heaven; but, nevertheless, even when his memory and heart are throbbing with recollections of that sublime scene, he says, "we have something surer still in the prophetic word." . . . It was not the miracles of Christ by which he came to know Jesus, but the word of Christ as interpreted by the spirit of Christ.[2]

Scripture is the product of God's Spirit moving upon its human authors to produce His Word in written form (2 Pet. 1:20–21). As such, it supersedes even apostolic experiences with Jesus Himself. Perhaps that is why Jesus prevented the disciples on the Emmaus Road from recognizing Him as He "explained to them the things concerning Himself in all the Scriptures" (Luke 24:27). He wanted their faith and preaching to be based on Scripture, not merely on their own personal experience—no matter how moving or memorable that experience might be. If that was true of the apostles, how much more should believers today seek to know God's Word rather than seeking supernatural or ecstatic experiences. Experience can be counterfeited easily, but not Scripture. It is once-for-all delivered!

God's sure Word makes the simple wise (v. 7). The Hebrew word translated "simple" comes from an expression meaning "an open door." It evokes the image of a naive person who doesn't know when to shut his mind to false or impure teaching. He is undiscerning, ignorant, and gullible. But God's Word makes him wise. "Wise" speaks not of one who merely knows some fact, but of one who is skilled in the art of godly living. He submits to Scripture and knows how to apply it to his circumstances. The Word of God thus takes a simple mind with no discernment and makes it skilled in all the issues of life. This, too, is in contrast to the wisdom of men, which in reality is foolishness (1 Cor. 1:20).

Scripture Is Right, Causing Joy. David adds a third statement about the Scripture's sufficiency. He writes, "The precepts of the Lord are right, rejoicing the heart." Precepts are divine principles and guidelines for character and conduct. Since God created us and knows how we must live to be productive for His glory, He has placed in Scripture every principle we need for godly living.

God's precepts, David said, are "right." Rather than simply indicating what is right as opposed to wrong, that word has the sense of showing someone the true path. The truths of Scripture lay out the proper path through the difficult maze of life. That's a wonderful confidence. So many people today are distressed or despondent because they lack direction and purpose. Most seek answers from the wrong sources. God's Word not only provides the light to our path (Ps. 119:105), but also sets the route before us.

Because it steers us through the right course of life, God's Word brings great joy. If you're depressed, anxious, fearful, or doubting, learn to obey God's counsel and share in the resulting delight. Don't turn to self-indulgent pursuits like self-esteem and self-fulfillment. Focus on divine truth. Therein you will find true and lasting joy. All other sources are shallow and fleeting.

The psalmist went to Scripture for help when he was discouraged or depressed. Psalm 119:50 says, "This is my comfort in my affliction, / That Thy word has revived me." Again, that speaks against the futility of the joyless paths men follow, pursuing happiness but never finding it to last.

Even the "weeping prophet" Jeremiah experienced joy amid tremendous human stress because God's Word was his joy and the delight of his heart (Jer. 15:16).

Scripture Is Pure, Enlightening the Eyes. Psalm 19:8 gives a fourth characteristic of Scripture's utter sufficiency: "The commandment of the Lord is pure, enlightening the eyes." "Commandment" stresses the Bible's non-optional nature. It is not a book of suggestions. Its divine mandates are authoritative and binding. Those who treat it lightly place themselves in eternal peril. Those who take it seriously find eternal blessing.

"Pure" could better be translated "lucid"—Scripture is not mystifying, confusing, or puzzling. The synonym "clear" is best. God's Word is a revelation—a revealing of truth to make the dark things light, bringing eternity into bright focus. Granted, there are things in Scripture that are hard to understand (2 Pet. 3:16). But taken as a whole, the Bible is not a bewildering book.

Scripture, because of its absolute clarity, brings understanding where there is ignorance, order where there is confusion, and light where there is spiritual and moral darkness. It stands in stark contrast to the muddled musings of unredeemed men, who themselves are blind and unable to discern truth or live righteously. God's Word clearly reveals the blessed, hopeful truths they can never see.

Scripture Is Clean, Enduring Forever. In Psalm 19:9 David uses the term "fear" as a synonym for God's Word: "The fear of the Lord is clean, enduring forever." "Fear" speaks of the reverential awe for God that compels us to worship Him. Scripture, in this sense, is God's manual on how to worship Him.

The Hebrew word translated "clean" speaks of the absence of impurity, filthiness, defilement, or imperfection. Scripture is without sin, evil, corruption, or error. The truth it conveys is therefore absolutely undefiled and without blemish. That truth is pictured in Psalm 12:6, where David calls the Word "flawless, like silver refined in a furnace of clay, purified seven times" (NIV).

Because it is flawless, Scripture endures forever (Ps. 19:9). Any change or modification could only introduce imperfection. Scripture is eternally and unalterably perfect. Jesus said, "Heaven and earth will pass away, but my words will not pass away" (Mark 13:31). That guarantees that the Bible is permanent, unchanging, and therefore relevant to everyone in every age of history. It has always been and will always be sufficient.

I once agreed to debate a man who led an "evangelical" homosexual denomination. I asked, "What do you do with the Bible's condemnations of homosexuality as sin?"

"Oh, come on!" he said. "Everybody knows that the Bible is psychologically unsophisticated, reflecting the views

of primitive thinking. The Bible is antiquated in its sociological theory. You can't go to an ancient document like
this and expect to deal with twentieth-century social problems. The Bible ought to stay in its own environment. It
needs to be updated with a contemporary understanding of
psychological and sociological phenomena."

It must grieve God when people slander Him by
claiming that the Bible is outdated or isn't sophisticated
enough for our educated society. Scripture needs no up-
dating, editing, or refining. Whatever time or culture you
live in, it is eternally relevant. It needs no help in that regard.
It is pure, sinless, inerrant truth; it is enduring. It is God's
revelation for every generation. It was written by the om-
niscient Spirit of God, who is infinitely more sophisticated
than anyone who dares stand in judgment on Scripture's
relevancy for our society, and infinitely wiser than all the
best philosophers, analysts, and psychologists who pass like
a childhood parade into irrelevancy.

Scripture Is True, Altogether Righteous. Verse 9 gives
the final characteristic and effect of God's all-sufficient Word:
"The judgments of the Lord are true; they are righteous
altogether." "Judgments" in that context means ordinances
or divine verdicts from the bench of the Supreme Judge of
the earth. The Bible is God's standard for judging the life
and eternal destiny of every person.

Unbelievers can't know what is true because they are
blind to God's Word. Being deceived by Satan, they search
vainly for spiritual truth. But aside from God's Word they
cannot discover ultimate truth about the things that really
matter: origins, the purpose of life, morality, values, life,
death, destiny, eternity, heaven, hell, true love, hope, security, and every other fundamental spiritual issue.

Recently I received a book on how to deal with depression, which was written by a contemporary psychiatrist. A section entitled "Reprogramming Your Conscious Mind" particularly caught my attention. The doctor's first suggestion was to shout, "Cancel!" every time you have a negative thought. She also recommended sleep programming—playing a tape recording all night that contains lots of positive feedback. During the day she said you should listen to positive music.

The doctor also thought it would be helpful to cultivate a meaningful spiritual philosophy. She said to find a belief system that works for you—any will do—but be sure to avoid people who talk about sin and guilt. Her final point was that you are to find the light in yourself. Unfortunately, that is the best human wisdom can do.[3]

Jesus illustrated the desperate, hopeless search for truth in human wisdom when He said to a group of unbelievers:

> Why do you not understand what I am saying? It is because you cannot hear My word. You are of your father the devil, and you want to do the desires of your father. He was a murderer from the beginning, and does not stand in the truth, because there is no truth in him. Whenever he speaks a lie, he speaks from his own nature; for he is a liar, and the father of lies. But because I speak the truth, you do not believe Me. . . . He who is of God hears the words of God; for this reason you do not hear them, because you are not of God. (John 8:43–47)

By way of contrast, believers have the truth about everything that really matters. What an enormous privilege to possess the Word of truth!

Because Scripture is true it is "righteous altogether" (Ps. 19:9). The implication of that phrase is that its truthfulness produces a comprehensive righteousness in those who accept it. And because it is a complete and exhaustive source of truth and righteousness, we are forbidden to add to it, take from it, or distort it in any way (Deut. 4:2; Rev. 22:18–19; 2 Pet. 3:15–16).

Psalm 119 gives further testimony to the righteous sufficiency of Scripture:

> Forever, O Lord,
> Thy word is settled in heaven.
>
> I esteem right all Thy precepts concerning everything,
> I hate every false way.
>
> Righteous art Thou, O Lord,
> And upright are Thy judgments.
> Thou hast commanded Thy testimonies in righteous-
> ness
> And exceeding faithfulness.
>
> Thy righteousness is an everlasting righteousness,
> And Thy law is truth.
>
> The sum of Thy word is truth,
> And every one of Thy righteous ordinances is everlast-
> ing. (vv. 89, 128, 137–38, 142, 160)

Contrary to what many are teaching today, there is no need for additional revelations, visions, or words of prophecy. In contrast to the theories of men, God's Word is true and absolutely comprehensive. Rather than seeking something more than God's glorious revelation, Christians need only to study and obey what they already have!

More Than Much Fine Gold

David concludes that God's Word is "more desirable than gold, yes, than much fine gold" (Ps. 19:10). Scripture is infinitely more precious than anything this world has to offer, perfectly sufficient for every need of life. Thus Scripture assesses its own immense value. As for its ability to satisfy our spiritual appetites, David writes that it is "sweeter also than honey and the drippings of the honeycomb." To David, meditating on God's Word was a source of great pleasure and enrichment. It meant more to him than the sweetest things in life.

Nothing this world has to offer is more precious than God's Word. I have a friend who collects rare Bibles. He owns a wonderful collection, with one Bible dating back to the fourth century. But my favorite is a Bible from sixteenth-century England, one of the earliest printed copies of God's Word. The top third of this Bible is covered with the blood of its original owner. My friend let me hold it in my hands, and tears came to my eyes as I leafed through it.

How did blood get on the pages of that Bible? When Bloody Mary ruled England, she terrorized Protestants, murdering as many as she could. Her soldiers would spill the person's blood, then take his Bible and dip it deep into the blood. A few of those Bibles have been preserved and are known as Martyrs' Bibles. Scientists have tested the paper and confirmed that the dark stains on every page of my friend's Bible are human blood.

I examined that Bible carefully, page by page. I could see where it was well worn from being studied. There are water stains, as if from tears, and places where a thumb had frayed favorite pages. This was someone's most valuable possession, and his or her blood is there to prove it.

In sad contrast, however, contemporary Christians tend to take their Bibles for granted, forgetting that many have given their lives just to own one copy. If the church today placed as high a value on God's Word as those martyrs did, perhaps there would not be so many people running off to experts in human theory and seeking counsel other than the perfect wisdom God gives us in His Word.

I am convinced that many who submit to various kinds of extrabiblical therapy do so precisely because they are looking for a way of solving their problems without surrendering to what they know God's Word requires of them.

Scripture hasn't failed them—they've failed Scripture. Many have never learned to let the Word of Christ richly dwell within them, as Paul instructs in Colossians 3:16. They have treated Scripture in a cursory way and never plumbed its depths. Their sinful neglect inevitably bears the fruit of doctrinal confusion and spiritual impotence. Because they never disciplined themselves to live according to biblical principles, they're now abandoning Scripture for worldly alternatives. They turn to psychoanalysis to solve their problems, to science to explain the origin of life, to philosophy to explain the meaning of life, and to sociology to explain why they sin. Churches, schools, and seminaries have thus made themselves vulnerable to the influence of such teachings.

In Psalm 19:11 David concludes his hymn on the sufficiency of Scripture: "Moreover, by [Thy judgments] Thy servant is warned; / In keeping them there is great reward."

89

The warnings of Scripture help to protect us against temptation, sin, error, foolishness, false teachers, and every other threat to our spiritual well-being. And to heed those warnings brings great reward. It is not a material prize; the Hebrew word for "reward" speaks of a spiritual blessing, not temporal riches. It is the settled joy and rest that come to those who live by God's Word.

There is no substitute for submission to Scripture. Your spiritual health depends on placing the utmost value on the Word of God and obeying it with an eager heart. If you think you can find answers to your spiritual problems through human counsel or worldly wisdom, you are forfeiting the most valuable and only reliable source of answers to the human dilemma. Don't relinquish the sweet, satisfying riches of God's Word for the bitter gall of this world's folly.

David ended this psalm by praying, "Let the words of my mouth and the meditation of my heart / Be acceptable in Thy sight, O Lord, my rock and my Redeemer" (v. 14). How can we be assured of having such acceptable thoughts and meditations? Joshua 1:8 gives us the answer and the results: "This book of the law shall not depart from your mouth, but you shall meditate on it day and night, so that you may be careful to do according to all that is written in it; for then you will make your way prosperous, and then you will have success."

5

Psychological
Sanctification?

How blessed is the man who does not walk in
the counsel of the wicked,
Nor stand in the path of sinners,
Nor sit in the seat of scoffers!
But his delight is in the law of the Lord,
And in His law he meditates day and night.

Psalm 1:1–2

Jesus said therefore to the twelve, "You do not want to go
away also, do you?" Simon Peter answered Him, "Lord, to
whom shall we go? You have words of eternal life."

John 6:67–68

RECENTLY SOMEONE SENT ME A BROCHURE advertising a seminar to teach hypnosis to clergymen. Among other things, the brochure said, "Hypnosis within the clergy is a natural. With the aid of hypnosis an individual will learn to maximize their own God-given abilities, and live healthier and happier lives." The brochure contained testimonies from ten people who had taken the class and felt it had enhanced their ministries.

Hypnosis, a form of shamanism made respectable by secular psychology, has not yet found widespread acceptance in the church. But if the people offering this seminar have their way, it is only a matter of time before evangelical pastors nationwide will be using post-hypnotic suggestion to "ensure a positive, permanent change after the therapy session has ended." How does that happen? "Hypnotherapy. . . allows the client's own inner mind to resolve conflicts," according to the brochure.

That is precisely what virtually every form of psychotherapy promises. Christian bookstores are full of books advising believers to "look deep within"; "get in touch with your inner self"; "explore the recesses of your past fears, hurts, and disappointments"; and "find the real answers to your problems within your own heart." Why? Because "the answers lie deep within."

Such advice sums up the very worst psychology offers. That it could be received and parroted by otherwise sound Christian leaders is tragic. Its influence on so many modern Christians is a serious threat to the church in our culture.

Nowhere does Scripture give such counsel. On the contrary, Scripture teaches us to "lay aside every encumbrance, and the sin which so easily entangles us, and . . . run with endurance the race that is set before us, *fixing our eyes on Jesus*, the author and perfecter of faith. . . . *Consider Him*" (Heb. 12:1–3, emphasis added). And, "Whatever is true, whatever is honorable, whatever is right, whatever is pure, whatever is lovely, whatever is of good repute, if there is any excellence and if anything worthy of praise, *let your mind dwell on these things*" (Phil. 4:8, emphasis added).

Can We Find Reliable Answers within Ourselves?

If we must look within and try to understand ourselves as a way of solving our problems, we are in a hopeless situation. Jeremiah 17:9–10 says, "The heart is more deceitful than all else / And is desperately sick; / Who can understand it? / I, the Lord, search the heart, / I test the mind." Problem-solving by self-examination results in deceitful answers. When we reach down inside ourselves to get answers, we get lies.

The sin in us is biased against God. Because of it our own heart lies to us about what we are really like. It exalts us in our own eyes, and absolves us of responsibility for sin. Proverbs 16:2 says, "All the ways of a man are clean in his own sight, / But the Lord weighs the motives," and Proverbs 14:12 says, "There is a way which seems right to a man, / But its end is the way of death."

Some might argue that those verses refer only to unbelievers. But even Christians are not immune from self-deceit. Paul said, "I am conscious of nothing against myself, yet I am not by this acquitted; but the one who examines me is the Lord" (1 Cor. 4:4). Paul couldn't find anything against himself, but he knew he couldn't rely only on his own self-examination.

We may reason that if we shouldn't trust ourselves, perhaps we can trust qualified counselors. But if we can't get truth out of our own hearts, how will someone else who also has a deceitful heart discern truth about us by putting us on a couch and listening? We can fool a therapist easier than we fool ourselves. While we sit trying to discover what's inside us, our hearts tell us lies. Can we expect a therapist to figure out the lies he or she is being told, and then tell us what we ought to do with our deceitful hearts? Whom are we kidding? Only God can test, evaluate, and know the truth of anyone's heart.

In Psalm 139:1–7 David prays,

O Lord, Thou hast searched me and known me.
Thou dost know when I sit down and when I rise up;
Thou dost understand my thought from afar.
Thou dost scrutinize my path and my lying down,
And art intimately acquainted with all my ways.

Even before there is a word on my tongue,
Behold, O Lord, Thou dost know it all.
Thou hast enclosed me behind and before,
And laid Thy hand upon me.
Such knowledge is too wonderful for me;
It is too high, I cannot attain to it.
Where can I go from Thy Spirit?

God doesn't get any skewed signals—He knows everything about you. If you want to get in touch with the real you, get in touch with the Holy Spirit as He applies the Word to your heart. Psalm 32:6–8 says,

Let everyone who is godly pray to Thee in a time when
    Thou mayest be found;
Surely in a flood of great waters they shall not reach him.
Thou art my hiding place; Thou dost preserve me from
    trouble;
Thou dost surround me with songs of deliverance.
I will instruct you and teach you in the way which you
    should go;
I will counsel you with My eye upon you.

Scripture does what psychoanalysis can't do: it pierces the heart. It penetrates deep into a person's soul and judges his motives. To see yourself in the light of Scripture is to see yourself as you really are. And only God's Word can promise real spiritual rewards to those who obey its counsel. No other form of therapy or counseling can make a person whole.

People say, "Oh, you have such a deep problem. You better go to a clinic somewhere for help, or get into psychotherapy, or find a deliverance ministry that can bind Satan and cast those demons out of you." Now please think carefully about this for a minute: what can those things add to the living, active, powerful Word of God? It is sharper than any other weapon. It will cut deeper and truer than anything that exists. Hebrews 4:12 declares that "the word of God is living and active and sharper than any two-edged sword, and piercing as far as the division of soul and spirit, of both joints and marrow, and able to judge the thoughts and intentions of the heart." As I have written elsewhere:

> God's Word is the perfect discerner, the perfect *kritikos* (from which we get "critic"). It not only analyzes all the facts perfectly, but all motives, and intentions, and beliefs as well, which even the wisest of human judges or critics cannot do. The sword of His Word will make no mistakes in judgment or execution.[1]

God's Word reveals the deepest thoughts and intentions of the human heart—so much so that "all things are open and laid bare to the eyes of Him with whom we have to do" (Heb. 4:13).

A Testimony about the Power of God's Word

I recently received this letter from a woman in our radio audience:

> I am a 27-year-old female. When I was 14, I began to experience depression frequently. I was not a Christian, nor was I raised by Christian parents. . . . My depression continued as I grew older, and as a result became worse as time passed. I became a chronic suicide case. . . .

When I was 20 I went to a psychiatrist, who diagnosed me as a manic depressive. He put me on lithium and told me I would be this way for the rest of my life. The drug therapy kept me from going into a severe suicidal depression. However, the deep feelings of depression and despair were still a reality.

I finally came so low that there was nowhere to turn but to the Lord. I heard the Christian life was supposed to be the only way to live, but God was not real to me. I decided I was going to seek God with my whole heart, as Jeremiah 29:13 says. Then if I found this to be nothing but an empty endeavor, I would give up living.

I fed upon tapes of your Bible teaching. The Lord began His work in me. Through His Word, as you taught, the Holy Spirit showed me just exactly what my problem was, and what I needed to do about it.

My problem was sin—a heart that would not forgive, and it was making me bitter. . . . I turned to the Lord and asked Him to help me forgive. I continued in the Word diligently, and the transformation process took place. The Lord delivered me from this depressive illness.

The memorizing of Scripture is renewing my mind. This is the only key for anyone suffering emotional problems, because it is the Living Word of God, it is the supernatural power to transform anyone's life and mind. . . . No doctor, no drugs can do what the Bible has done for me in changing my life.

Then she added a P.S.:

By the way, I have been off all medication for three years now! Obedience is the key!

I believe that testimony. I believe in the power of God's Word. And I grieve that so many seeking people are diverted into humanistic psychology and psychiatry, which only compounds their problems by moving them the wrong direction—away from the sufficiency of Christ and the power of His Word.

Becoming People of the Word

James 1:25 says, "One who looks intently at the perfect law, the law of liberty, and abides by it, not having become a forgetful hearer but an effectual doer, this man shall be blessed in what he does."

The phrase "looks intently" translates the Greek word *parakuptō*, which literally means "to stoop over" or "to bend down to examine something with care and precision." It pictures both the humble attitude and the intense study required of one who seeks to benefit from the "perfect law" (a synonym for God's Word).

The Greek word translated "perfect" speaks of completeness or wholeness. As we have seen, God's Word is sufficient, comprehensive, completely without error, and able to meet every need and fulfill the desires of every heart. If we obey it, we will be blessed in whatever we do.

What a glorious treasure God has given us in His Word! How should Christians respond to it? Psalm 19:14 records David's response: "Let the words of my mouth and the meditation of my heart / Be acceptable in Thy sight, / O Lord, my rock and my Redeemer." In other words, "May the things I think and the things I say be acceptable to you. May they be consistent with Your Word." David prayed that he would be a man of the Word, with biblical thoughts and words.

Even more direct and comprehensive are Paul's statements to the Ephesian elders in Acts 20:

> I did not shrink from declaring to you anything that was profitable, and teaching you publicly and from house to house. . . . I did not shrink from declaring to you the whole purpose of God. . . . And now I commend you to God and to the word of His grace, which is able to build you up and to give you the inheritance among all those who are sanctified. (vv. 20, 27, 32)

Those elders were just like us. They had all the basic problems, struggles, and spiritual needs we have. From the first day Paul set foot in Asia he began to teach them God's Word (vv. 18–19). He held nothing back because it all was profitable for them. He saw in divine revelation total sufficiency for every struggle, need, and anxiety of human life. When he left them, he commended them to God and the Word of His grace, which he knew would edify and strengthen them for faithful service.

Spiritual leaders must once again embrace the sufficiency of Scripture and call their people back to it. Individual Christians must covenant with God to be men and women of the Word, finding their resources there and applying them to every aspect of their lives. You'll never know what the Word can do if you don't study and apply it. It isn't enough to simply say you believe it. It must occupy an exalted place in your life. Since God Himself exalts it and magnifies it (Ps. 138:2), how much more should we?

As noted at the end of the last chapter, Joshua 1:8 sums up the absolute sufficiency of God's Word as our guide for successful living: "This book of the law shall not depart from your mouth, but you shall meditate on it day and night, so that you may be careful to do according to all that is written in it; for then you will make your way prosperous, and then you will have success."

Counseling with the Bible

We all participate in the counseling process when we instruct one another from God's Word, intercede in prayer, and are used by the Holy Spirit to help the weak and heavy-hearted (1 Thess. 5:14). The importance of that ministry was impressed on my heart again recently when I spoke with a dear Christian lady who has a terminal illness and is near death. I know she loves the Lord and has committed her life to Him. Her greatest desire is to obey His will. But she told me that she lives in constant fear of going to hell. When I asked her why she was so afraid, she said, "When I first got this disease, I did a terrible, terrible thing. I used profane words and cursed God. Now I'm afraid He won't forgive me and I'm going to go to hell for what I did." I could see she was deeply troubled by what she had done.

What do you say to a person like that? Death may be only days away and she needs assurance of God's forgiveness. Do you send her for psychoanalysis? Or bind the demon of doubt? Or tell her to visualize herself in heaven? Or coach her through six or seven stages of personal discovery therapy? That's what many are advocating today.

No, you don't do any of those things. Someone like that needs reassurance from Scripture about God's love and forgiveness, so the Spirit can impress that truth on her heart and give her peace. I took her through passages of Scripture that speak of the complete forgiveness that belongs to every believer. I assured her that even though she had cursed God, there was someone who blasphemed God far more, and he received abundant grace and forgiveness. I read Paul's testimony to her from 1 Timothy 1:12–16:

> I thank Christ Jesus our Lord, who has strengthened me, because He considered me faithful, putting me into service; even though I was formerly a blasphemer and a persecutor and a violent aggressor. And yet I was shown mercy, because I acted ignorantly in unbelief; and the grace of our Lord was more than abundant, with the faith and love which are found in Christ Jesus.
>
> It is a trustworthy statement, deserving full acceptance, that Christ Jesus came into the world to save sinners, among whom I am foremost of all.
>
> And yet for this reason I found mercy, in order that in me as the foremost, Jesus Christ might demonstrate His perfect patience, as an example for those who would believe in Him for eternal life.

I reminded her that Paul's testimony was an example to the whole world that since God could save the chief sinner, He can save all the lesser ones too—including her. As we continued to talk and pray together, there was great hope in her voice.

The answer for people with that kind of anxiety is simply to open to them the Word of the living God and allow the Holy Spirit to apply it to the heart. Even someone on the threshold of death can know the blessing of peace and confidence that comes from God's Word.

Counseling and encouraging one another with the Bible has always played an important role in the church. That role wasn't given to Christian psychologists or secular psychoanalysts. It was given to pastors and teachers, and through their careful proclamation and instruction, to spiritually gifted Christians whose lives are pure, whose knowledge of God's Word is mature, and who are available channels of the Word, the Spirit, and divine wisdom. Paul said to the Roman believers, "You . . . are full of goodness, filled with all knowledge, and able also to admonish one another" (Rom. 15:14).

Each Christian is called to help, stimulate, and encourage one another within the body of Christ (Heb. 10:24–25). We must not allow neo-gnostic error to steal that ministry from those proficient in the Word and give it instead to professionals who adulterate it by mixing it with human wisdom and psychological theory.

Whatever Happened to the Holy Spirit?

Before we move away from the subject of psychology, we need to note its catastrophic effect on the church's understanding of the Holy Spirit's ministry. When our Lord's crucifixion was drawing near, He promised to send "another Helper . . . that is the Spirit of truth" (John 14:16–17). That was His promise that the Holy Spirit would assume the same role He had filled in His disciples' lives for the years of His earthly ministry—that of divine teacher, friend, guide, helper, and comforter. The Holy Spirit's ministry in that regard is one of the wonderful resources Christ has made available to all who know Him. The apostle Paul wrote, "We have received, not the spirit of the world, but the Spirit who is from God, that we might know the things freely given to us by God" (1 Cor. 2:12). All spiritual wisdom and resources come from the Holy Spirit. We may simply turn to Him if we want to know the truth about ourselves and the solutions to our problems. Tragically, the current neglect of the Spirit's ministries has greatly crippled many Christians' willingness and ability to do so.

In the early years of my ministry I traveled around the country preaching at many churches, Bible conferences, and camps. Almost everywhere I went people wanted to hear a message about the Holy Spirit. They wanted to know about spiritual gifts and what it meant to walk by the Spirit and be filled with the Spirit. Books and seminars on those topics were hot items. "Spirit-filled" was the catchphrase of the entire evangelical movement. But in recent years that has changed considerably. Now the Spirit's ministries as outlined in the holy book seem to have been de-emphasized almost to the point of neglect.

I think part of the blame for that situation must fall on the charismatic movement's misrepresentations of the baptism, filling, and illuminating work of the Spirit. Their overemphasis on miracles, signs, and wonders has misrepresented the Holy Spirit as some sort of divine magician who moves in ways that are always seen, felt, or heard. They have downplayed the Spirit's internal sanctifying work, which is the essence of His ministry. Many Christians are unwilling to confront the excesses of the charismatic movement or even to speak on the subject of the Spirit's ministries for fear of offending someone who holds a different view. Those who do speak out are often branded unloving or divisive. Consequently, many non-charismatic pastors and teachers avoid the subject of the Holy Spirit altogether, and that has led to widespread ignorance about His ministries.

Unfamiliarity with the Spirit's sanctifying work has opened the door for the church's current obsession with psychology. Psychological sanctification has become a substitute for the Spirit-filled life. What point is there in seeking the Holy Spirit's comfort if, after all, deep-seated emotional problems can be addressed only by a trained psychologist, or if people can come to grips with their lives only by getting in touch with their childhood, or if the answers to our deepest hurts are buried deep within us? If those things are true, we don't need an Advocate; we need a therapist. And that is precisely the route many in the church have chosen.

I recently received the following letter from a woman in our radio audience. She had listened to a portion of the broadcasts we had titled "Whatever Happened to the Holy Spirit?" and wrote to disagree with my comments about psychotherapy. Her views are representative of what many contemporary Christians believe:

> I have never agreed with your view of psychologists and how you lump them all together, Christian and secular. A recent awareness of past events has made this all the more disturbing. I wonder if you realize the harm you are doing as you turn people who have deep emotional problems away from seeking the help they need.
>
> If you came from an ideal family situation you may well have difficulty understanding how deeply the spirits of some people have been wounded and how it has warped the very fiber of their being. Oftentimes the incidents have been sublimated by the youngster only to surface as an adolescent or adult. Recommending only Bible study and prayer can be like putting on a Band-Aid when you need surgery. Just becoming a

Christian doesn't solve the dilemma, either (I used to think it does), because the troubled person may just consider their past life experiences fairly normal, having sublimated the deep hurt of their spirit. Then because these matters have never been dealt with they carry them on into their marriages and then begins another cycle.

The woman added some personal details about a son-in-law who she felt needed psychological counseling. He was being abusive to his wife and had even threatened to kill her. He refused to accept responsibility for his wrong behavior, always finding ways to blame others for things that were wrong in his own life. The entire family had been encouraging him to seek psychological counseling for more than a year but he had refused. Now he was using my teaching as justification for his refusal to seek a therapist's help. She closed with these comments:

> The simplistic answer is that it's due to sin: ask God to forgive you, forgive others, read your Bible and pray. Ask God to help you do better. But you also have to address what the sin has done and if the person is not aware of the problem that has become so deeply buried in their subconscious, how are they going to go about correcting it? A man with a broken leg isn't helped by rubbing ointment on the hurting area. Until you discover the underlying cause of the pain, you can't bring about healing.
>
> The Christian psychologist has been trained and is better able to get to the root of these serious problems . . . a friend or good listener isn't of much help because the matter is too deep, and a minister has an entire congregation to minister to. How in the world could he justify the time it would take to deal with just a few in

his congregation? Life is becoming more complex and relationships more fragile because of it AND YOU DON'T THINK CHRISTIANS SHOULD SEEK PROFESSIONAL COUNSELING???? I wonder how many other needy people have been persuaded not to seek professional help they desperately need. I shudder to think of the responsibility that is yours as your voice travels the airways, discouraging people from getting the help they need.

I sincerely hope that we have misunderstood the real meaning of what you meant. . . . To make my point very clear: I DO NOT AGREE WITH YOU THAT CHRISTIANS SHOULD NOT SEEK PROFESSIONAL PSYCHOLOGICAL COUNSELING. If the need is there, they should avail themselves of the help.

I sympathize with that dear woman's plight. She is desperately seeking help for her daughter's marriage and is even concerned for the daughter's physical safety. She hints that her grandchildren's behavior is being adversely affected by the trouble in the home. She is frustrated by her son-in-law's hypocrisy; evidently he maintains a front of spirituality by reading his Bible and praying regularly. But his private life is undisciplined and often grossly unrighteous. Something is terribly wrong. If her description of the situation is accurate, I entirely agree that her son-in-law desperately needs help. And I would admonish him to seek wise counsel—urgently.

But is this woman encouraging him to seek answers from the right source? Is her view of his spiritual and emotional condition shaped by biblical understanding, or by the theories of modern psychology? Note her presuppositions: She has concluded that deep emotional problems like those of her son-in-law require some remedy Scripture and prayer can't possibly provide. She believes, in fact, that Bible study and prayer are superficial, "Band-Aid" solutions, and that only psychotherapy offers meaningful help for people with such problems. She assumes that most emotional problems are rooted in childhood wounds and that the causes of emotional injuries are usually sublimated and require professional therapy to bring them to the surface. She evidently believes the only true "professional" counselors are those trained in psychotherapy. She says it is "simplistic" to suppose that her son-in-law's behavior is due to sin—or to view repentance as any kind of solution. Complex emotional problems, she believes, can be unscrambled only by professionals trained to delve into the subconscious mind. Those disorders are evidently "too deep" for biblical wisdom and need the insight of someone with a higher wisdom than Scripture offers—someone equipped with better resources than the Bible, prayer, and the Holy Spirit to deal with the complexities of our age.

Not one of those presuppositions is in harmony with what the New Testament teaches about sanctification. Far from being a superficial remedy, God's Word is the *only* tool adequate for radical surgery on the human soul: It is "living and active and sharper than any two-edged sword, and piercing as far as the division of soul and spirit, of both joints and marrow, and able to judge the thoughts and intentions of the heart" (Heb. 4:12). Modern behavioral science, by comparison, is superficial—and usually downright counterproductive.

More important, sanctification is the Holy Spirit's role. No therapist can accomplish what He can do in transforming the soul. And no therapy devised by men can possibly bring someone to repentance or repair the life broken by sin. Those who see therapy as the best means to cure a sick or wounded soul are trying to substitute fleshly devices for the work of the Spirit.

Are You Now Being Perfected by the Flesh?

Scripture speaks pointedly to this very issue. The Galatian church initially trusted in God for their salvation, yet foolishly compromised the gospel of grace by relying on human effort for personal holiness and spiritual maturity. In Galatians 3:1–5 Paul says,

> You foolish Galatians, who has bewitched you, before whose eyes Jesus Christ was publicly portrayed as crucified? This is the only thing I want to find out from you: did you receive the Spirit by the works of the Law, or by hearing with faith? Are you so foolish? Having begun by the Spirit, *are you now being perfected by the flesh?*
> Did you suffer so many things in vain—if indeed it was in vain? Does He then, who provides you with the Spirit and works miracles among you, do it by the works of the Law, or by hearing with faith? (emphasis added)

In verse 1 Paul describes the Galatians as "foolish" (in Greek, *anoētos*), which indicates an absence of wisdom or perception. He wasn't saying they lacked intelligence. He was rebuking them for failing to use their intelligence to apply the truth they knew. They had been disobedient to what they knew and were therefore being spiritually reckless. They had sinfully neglected their spiritual resources and tried to substitute fleshly formulae—exactly like many Christians today.

The J. B. Phillips translation of Galatians 3:1 says, "Oh you dear idiots of Galatia."[2] *The Jerusalem Bible* is even more graphic: "Are you people in Galatia mad?"[3]

Paul told the Galatians they were doctrinally vulnerable, having been "bewitched" (in Greek, *baskainō*) by false teachers who told them they could achieve sanctification by their own efforts. In its strict sense *baskainō* speaks of casting a magic spell or seeking to bring harm to a person through an evil eye or a spoken word. Paul didn't mean the Galatians were victims of sorcery or other occult activities. He meant they had been charmed or fascinated by evil teachers.

The situation at Galatia is typical of Satan's efforts to defuse the Spirit's power in believers' lives. Whenever grace is received, he attempts to pervert it with legalism. Whenever faith is exercised, he attempts to replace it with works. Paul had preached to the Galatians a gospel of justification by faith and sanctification by the Holy Spirit; but the Judaizers (Jewish false teachers) wanted to add law to grace and works to faith. They sought to impose upon the Galatian Christians the rituals, ceremonies, laws, and legalism of Judaism. It was a subtle, satanic attack in religious trappings, and the Galatians were willing victims.

The answer to Paul's rhetorical question in verse 2 is obvious: the Galatians had received the Spirit by faith, not by works. They received Him at the same time they received salvation. In fact, the witness of the Spirit is the greatest proof we have of our salvation. He bears witness with our spirit that we are children of God and joint heirs with Christ (Rom. 8:16–17). His presence in our lives is the unmistakable evidence of God's favor.

The infusion of psychotherapy into Christian counseling today smacks of Galatianism. It is little more than a systematic effort to eliminate the Holy Spirit from sanctification. It might be more subtle than the legalistic attacks of the first-century Judaizers, but it nonetheless poses the same monumental threat to the church.

For many, self-esteem, self-worth, and a man-centered theology have created a greater confidence in self than in the Holy Spirit. The truth is, only the Holy Spirit can produce and sustain spiritual life. Apart from Him, all our efforts are in vain. If He ever ceased His sanctifying, sustaining work within us, we would fall back into spiritual deadness. We live by the Spirit (Gal. 5:25). And what He provides is ample for every need—the all-sufficient Spirit supplies the necessary resources for every issue of life.

Don't be victimized. The church today is filled with sin and weakness because many Christians have forgotten that spiritual warfare is fought with spiritual weapons (1 Cor. 10:4), not fleshly techniques, theories, and therapies. Sanctification comes by the Spirit working through the Word to transform us into Christ's image (2 Cor. 3:18).

Therefore we must reject man-centered, humanistic "solutions" and learn to rely on the Spirit and walk in His power. Perfecting spirituality in the flesh didn't work for the Galatians and it won't work for us. As God Himself said long ago, it is "not by might nor by power, but by My Spirit" (Zech. 4:6).

Where can we get reliable answers for life's hardest questions? Our all-sufficient Savior has not left us without ample spiritual resources. His perfect wisdom is available through His Word. Comfort, assurance, understanding, and power are ours through the ministry of His indwelling Spirit. All of that is amplified by loving ministry from gifted people who operate in the community of believers. And it all works together to assure that each believer has perfect "abundance for every good deed" (2 Cor. 9:8).

6

Bible-Believing Doubters

All Scripture is inspired by God and profitable for teaching, for reproof, for correction, for training in righteousness; that the man of God may be adequate, equipped for every good work.

2 Timothy 3:16–17

Preach the word; be ready in season and out of season; reprove, rebuke, exhort, with great patience and instruction. For the time will come when they will not endure sound doctrine; but wanting to have their ears tickled, they will accumulate for themselves teachers in accordance to their own desires; and will turn away their ears from the truth, and will turn aside to myths.

2 Timothy 4:2–4

RECENTLY I HAD THE PRIVILEGE OF PREACHING in the Sunday morning worship service of the Central Baptist Church in Kiev, USSR. It was one of the most moving experiences of my life. The converted house was crammed with hundreds of people sitting and standing wall to wall. More were on a porch peering through open windows into the main room. Even more were outside surrounding the building and looking (if they could find a path of clear vision) toward the pulpit while listening to outdoor speakers.

The people were reverent, subdued, and prayerful as the service unfolded. The volunteer choir, dressed in common clothes, sang several anthems of praise. Most people, even those inside, kept their overcoats on because of the cold. The congregation sang hymns from memory (no hymnals) and there were spontaneous times of impassioned weeping and sobbing prayer for the lost.

The pastor asked me to bring the third message of the morning (the third one is always the main one) and then call for people who wished to repent and follow Jesus Christ to come to the platform (the Soviet Christians all use the term *repenting* to describe their salvation).

When I finished preaching on Psalm 19, and the sufficiency of Scripture, two hours of the service had gone by. I simply asked those who wanted to repent of their sins and follow Jesus Christ in faith, to work their way up to the platform to greet the elders.

Immediately people began to come. Most were weeping. The crowd smoothly adjusted so they could find their way through. As they came, many touched them, hugged them, and squeezed their hands and arms. There was an audible murmur of tearful prayer.

One and a half hours later, the last person had come and the final hymn was sung.

There had been no coercing, no mood music, no manipulation, and no prodding—just a quiet waiting as people came.

Most heartwarming of all was what happened when the repenters reached the little platform. They were told to kneel before the people and the elders, a microphone was held to their mouths, and they were asked to repent of their sins and confess Jesus as Lord so that all could hear. Each one did that. Humbly, broken in spirit, desperate for salvation, and with no sense of self-consciousness because of the humbling work of the Spirit, they publicly turned from sin to follow the Lord Jesus Christ.

Rejoicing and weeping ran through all of this. People were embracing those to be received into the body of Christ.

The service ended when a precious young girl quoted a poem and three little girls sang a song of love to Jesus.

116

There was no entertainment, no clever techniques, no effort to make salvation easy, no attempt to maneuver the crowd, no superficial performances—the Word of God had been preached (three times) and people prayed for its power to be released. I felt I was in the Book of Acts with the early church and didn't want to leave!

The Word had done its work, and I knew again why Satan will do everything he can to replace the powerful Word of God in the life of the church.

Precisely because it is so powerful, the Bible has always had its enemies. Unbelievers challenge its credibility. Skeptics question its accuracy. Moral revisionists depreciate its precepts. Religious liberals dispute its supernatural character. Cultists twist its meaning.

The most dangerously effective assault on God's Word, however, may be a subtle one that has been fostered primarily by those who think of themselves as Bible believers—but who doubt the perfect sufficiency of Scripture.

Contemporary evangelicalism has been beguiled and sabotaged by a ruinous lack of confidence in God's Word. I'm not talking about the question of whether God gave us an inerrant Bible. Of course He did. And the great majority of evangelicals accept that without question. But many who would never doubt the Bible's authenticity as God's Word or distrust its essential authority as a guide for righteous living have nevertheless accepted the notion that Scripture simply does not contain *all* we need to minister well in these complex and sophisticated modern times. So they turn to human expertise in the fields of psychology, business, government, politics, entertainment, or whatever else they think might supply some recipe for success that's lacking in Scripture.

That perspective denies the glorious truth of the verses I've quoted at the beginning of this chapter. Most Christians are familiar with 2 Timothy 3:16—a key passage on inspiration: "All Scripture is inspired by God and profitable for teaching, for reproof, for correction, for training in righteousness." There Scripture claims to be the very breath of God ("inspired," *theopneustos* in Greek, means "God-breathed"). But don't miss the next verse. It tells us that the Bible is adequate to equip believers for *every* good work. Because Scripture ties these two claims together, it is either wholly inspired *and* wholly sufficient, or it is not inspired at all.

Digging a bit deeper into this crucial text will reveal that the term "man of God" is a technical one used frequently in the Old Testament to refer to one who spoke for God—a prophet, a preacher. Paul is saying that Timothy, who was just such a "man of God," called to be perfectly equipped for every good work was to find his complete sufficiency through the Word.

Further, it was Timothy's duty and the duty of all preachers to teach, reprove, correct, and train in righteousness—all of which can only be done in the application of the sufficient, inspired Scripture.

Those two verses tell us pointedly that the man of God must be committed to the Word of God.

A Blueprint for Disaster

Once at a pastors' conference a man asked me, "What's the real secret of Grace Community Church's vitality and growth?"

I said, "The clear and forceful teaching of the Word."

I was shocked when he countered, "Don't give me that! I tried it and it doesn't work. What's the *real* secret?"

I knew enough about that pastor to be certain that if you asked him whether he believed in the sufficiency of Scripture, he would have said yes. But what he professes to believe doesn't work its way into his philosophy of ministry. He presumes that to build his church effectively he needs some gimmick, an inventive strategy, or a more up-to-date methodology. He is trying to supplement the imagined inadequacies of God's Word. Probably without realizing it, he has concluded that the Bible alone is an inadequate resource for ministry, and he's looking for something else to fill the gap.

Another Christian leader was quoted as saying he believes there will never be a revival in America until we have a Christian Congress. He has left the pastorate and is now working to get Christians elected to office. He supposes he can accomplish through politics what he will never accomplish through teaching the Word of God. He would probably lay his life on the line for the truthfulness of Scripture. But for some reason he does not believe preaching it to people can have as great an impact as political action.

Can politics achieve spiritual results the Bible can't? In Nehemiah's day it was the Word of God that prompted a national revival (Nehemiah 8). Is Scripture somehow less effective than it was then? No doubt my friend would verbally affirm the full authority, potency, and sufficiency of the Bible. But in practice he has capitulated to the trend-setters who feel something extra is needed.

I see the same trend more and more in otherwise solid churches. Pastors are turning to textbooks on secular management theory for help. They view the non-Christian

119

CEO of a multinational corporation as a role model—as if the fads of secular business provided more important guidelines for building God's kingdom than Scripture. But the business world is preoccupied with image and profit, not truth. Unfortunately, the church has absorbed that warped sense of priorities. Christian leaders seem obsessed with promoting church growth through human ingenuity. Often they are more versed in current management theory than in biblical theology. Yet Scripture says it is the Lord who adds to the church (Acts 2:47), not men. Christ said *He* would build His church (Matt. 16:18). The means of legitimate church growth are all supernatural, because the church is supernatural. Why should we add human methodology to what our Lord is doing to build the church?

I am convinced that Christians who search beyond Scripture for ministry strategies inevitably end up opposing Christ's work, albeit unwittingly. We don't need to pick through this world's tainted wisdom to sort out new insights or answers for spiritual issues. The only reliable answers are there for us in the Bible. That's true not just in the area of counseling, as we have seen, but also in matters such as evangelism, spiritual growth, church leadership, and other issues Christians must understand if they are to minister effectively. Scripture is the only perfect blueprint for all true ministry, and those who build according to any other plan are erecting a structure that will be unacceptable to the Master Architect.

What More Can Be Said?

Am I writing off every source of extrabiblical help as utterly worthless? Are there *no* beneficial insights to be gained by looking at the observations of sociologists and psychologists? Are there *no* helpful principles church leaders might learn from secular management experts? Are there *no* techniques pastors can legitimately employ from a specialist's empirical observations of church growth? Is there *nothing* to be learned outside the Bible itself that can be useful in the church?

Useful, perhaps. Necessary, no. If they are necessary, they are in Scripture. Otherwise, God has left us short of what we need, and that would be unthinkable. Human ingenuity occasionally intersects with truth. Even a stopped clock is right twice a day. But that is poor performance compared to Scripture, which is true in all its assertions and sufficient for the life and growth of the church.

Certainly there is nothing wrong with a pastor reading secular books on relationships or management and implementing a helpful suggestion he might find there. But if he is studying such things because he thinks he might uncover some great, indispensable secret Scripture doesn't reveal about how to cure the ills of the soul or how to lead a church, then he has a low view of the Bible's sufficiency. If he bases his work on the secular suggestions, he will probably devise an unbiblical system of evangelism, counseling, and church leadership.

Similarly, a pastor might legitimately study oratory to hone his preaching skills; or a church musician might study techniques for singing more expressively. Believers in ministry can certainly glean useful helps from that kind of learning. But anyone who thinks better technique can add an ounce of power to the biblical message has an inadequate understanding of the sufficiency of God's Word.

I met a man who left the church where he was minister of music to go into show business. He told me, "I've learned one thing: you can't just get up there and give people the gospel. You've got to have a platform. You've got to have people's respect. If I can become famous and use my status as a star to give people the gospel, just imagine how powerful the message would be!"

My response was that the message couldn't be any more powerful than it already is, and one's power in presenting it has nothing to do with being a celebrity. The gospel is "the power of God for salvation to everyone who believes" (Rom. 1:16). What was this would-be superstar saying? Does he believe the poor gospel limps along until we give it credibility—and that we do so by fame, not virtue, by technique, not the power of God's Spirit?

How did the early Church ever function without the "expertise" we have today? Yet those Christians turned the world upside down (Acts 17:6), and they did it without any celebrity testimonies, without modern management techniques, without psychotherapy, without mass media, and without most of the means the contemporary church seems to view as essential. All they had was God's Word and the power of His Spirit, but they knew that was sufficient.

How has the pure, humble, devout church behind the Iron Curtain for most of this century been so powerful without the marketing strategies of the West?

I fear that in the Western world, churches and Christian leaders who hold uncompromisingly to the Bible's sufficiency are rapidly becoming a thing of the past. J. I. Packer saw this trend years ago and wrote,

> The outside observer sees us as staggering on from gimmick to gimmick and stunt to stunt like so many drunks in a fog, not knowing at all where we are or

which way we should be going. Preaching is hazy; heads are muddled; hearts fret; doubts drain strength; uncertainty paralyses action. . . . Unlike the first Christians who in three centuries won the Roman world, and those later Christians who pioneered the Reformation, and the Puritan awakening and the Evangelical revival, and the great missionary movement of the last century, we lack certainty.[1]

The church lacks certainty because it has adopted an improper view of Scripture. Evidently many Christians no longer believe that the Bible is the all-sufficient guidebook for the life and conduct of the church.

What the Divine Author Says

To counter that trend, we must understand what God has revealed about the utter sufficiency of Scripture and let it determine our ministry philosophy. Anything less denies God His proper place as the sovereign authority in our lives and ministries.

Paul underscores the complete sufficiency of Scripture in 2 Timothy 3:16, showing four ways God has testified that His Word is wholly adequate for every spiritual need:

Scripture Teaches Truth. The Bible is first of all profitable for teaching. The Greek word translated "teaching" (*didaskalia*) has primary reference to the *content* of teaching rather than the *process* of teaching. That is, Scripture is the operational manual of divine truth that must govern our lives.

Every Christian has the spiritual capacity to receive and respond to Scripture. Non-Christians lack this receptivity to biblical truth: "A natural man does not accept the things of the Spirit of God; for they are foolishness to him, and he cannot understand them, because they are spiritually appraised" (1 Cor. 2:14). The Christian, by way of contrast, has "the mind of Christ" (v. 16). The Holy Spirit enables him or her to apprehend God's Word with spiritual discernment, wisdom, and understanding. No Christian lacks that ability; each one possesses the Holy Spirit as a resident Teacher of truth (1 John 2:27).

In the practical sense, our holiness is directly proportional to our knowledge of and consequent obedience to God's Word. The psalmist said, "Thy word I have treasured in my heart, / That I may not sin against Thee" (Ps. 119:11). The more complete our working knowledge of the Bible is, the less susceptible we are to sin and error. The Lord says in Hosea 4:6, "My people are destroyed for lack of knowledge." Having rejected true knowledge, they were unable to live as God wanted them to live. Theirs was a willful disregard for God's Word—but neglect or complacency have the same destructive effect.

The best way to avoid serious spiritual problems, therefore, is to give yourself to the faithful, patient, and thorough study of Scripture with an obedient heart—"for then you will make your way prosperous, and then you will have success" (Josh. 1:7–8).

Scripture Reproves Sin and Error. Scripture is also profitable for reproof (2 Tim. 3:16). It confronts and rebukes misconduct and false teaching. According to Archbishop Richard Trench, to reprove is "so to rebuke another, with such effectual wielding of the victorious arm of the truth, as to bring him, if not always to a confession, yet at least to a conviction, of his sin."[2] Scripture has that effect on us as we study it and feel its convicting power, or on others as we point them to it.

Two aspects of reproof are evident in Scripture: reproof of sinful conduct and reproof of erroneous teaching. Paul instructed Timothy, who was trying to clean up the church at Ephesus, "Preach the word; be ready in season and out of season; reprove, rebuke, exhort" (2 Tim. 4:2). The primary purpose he had in view was reproof of sinful conduct. Timothy was to preach and apply Scripture so that people would turn from sin and walk in holiness—even though the time would come when most people would never tolerate such preaching (v. 3).

Hebrews 4:12–13 also speaks of reproving sinful conduct. Verse 12 pictures God's Word as a two-edged sword that cuts deep into a person's being to expose and judge his innermost thoughts and motives. Verse 13 says, "There is no creature hidden from His sight, but all things are open and laid bare to the eyes of Him with whom we have to do." God penetrates our hearts with His Word and lays us open before His eyes.

The Greek word translated "laid bare" in that verse was used of criminals who were being led to trial or execution. Often a soldier would hold the point of a dagger under the criminal's chin to force him to hold his head high so everyone could see who he was. Similarly, Scripture exposes us for who we really are and forces us to face the reality of our sin.

Perhaps you've had times when you've drifted into spiritual complacency and felt content in your sin, only to have God's Word cut deep into your heart with overwhelming conviction. That's the reproving power of Scripture, and it's a precious blessing.

A good way to ensure that our churches don't become havens for willful sinners is for pastors to preach the Word faithfully and accurately. Christians will be convicted of their sins and most unbelievers will either repent or leave. Few people will allow themselves to be exposed to the reproof of God's Word week after week if they have no desire for holiness. Jesus said evildoers hate the light and don't come to it so their deeds won't be exposed (John 3:20). Making unbelievers and evildoers feel welcome and comfortable in the church by non-confrontive, vapid, shallow preaching leads them to false security on the basis of their attendance, participation, religious feelings, and acceptance. That can be a damning deceit.

Scripture, as the standard by which all claims to truth must be tested, also reproves erroneous teaching. The apostle John reveals the power of the Word as truth when he says that believers who overcome the evil one do so because "[they] are strong and the Word of God abides in [them]" (1 John 2:14). The evil one, Satan, works through false religion (2 Cor. 11:14) but is ineffective with those who are strong in the Word. That's why the cults attempt to discredit, distort, or supplant Scripture with their own writings. Since the Bible shows their errors for what they are, they must change its meaning to justify themselves. However, those who tamper with Scripture do so "to their own destruction" (2 Pet. 3:16).

Christians who have a thorough grasp of biblical truth are not like undiscerning infants, but like strong young men who can easily recognize false teachings and avoid being "children, tossed here and there by waves, and carried about by every wind of doctrine, by the trickery of men, by craftiness in deceitful scheming" (Eph. 4:14).

Scripture Corrects Behavior. Scripture is also profitable for correction (2 Tim. 3:16). It not only exposes sinful behavior and erroneous teaching, but also corrects them. The Greek word translated "correction" (*epanorthōsis*) literally means "to straighten up" or "lift up." In other words, Scripture restores us to a proper spiritual posture.

I regularly experience that, don't you? Scripture will pierce my heart and bring conviction, but then it gives me instruction so I can correct the sin. It doesn't leave me stranded spiritually. As we allow the Word to richly dwell within us (Col. 3:16), it builds us up (Acts 20:32) and transforms our weaknesses into strengths.

There is a purifying, cleansing aspect to the Bible's corrective power. Jesus said, "You are already clean because of the word which I have spoken to you" (John 15:3). No humanly conceived method of therapy and no program yet devised by any expert can have that corrective, purifying effect. But every Christian has experienced it. It is one more evidence of the perfect sufficiency of the resources we inherit in Christ.

Scripture Trains in Righteousness. Training in righteousness (2 Tim. 3:16) is another process by which God's Word transforms our thinking and behavior.

The Greek word translated "training" is *paidion*, which elsewhere in the New Testament is translated "child" or "children" (for example, see Matt. 2:8; 14:21). So this verse pictures God's Word training believers as a parent or teacher would train a child. From spiritual infancy to spiritual maturity, Scripture trains and educates believers in godly living.

Scripture is the Christian's spiritual nourishment. In 1 Timothy 4:6 Paul instructs Timothy to be "constantly nourished on the words of the faith and of . . . sound doctrine." In Matthew 4:4 Jesus says, "Man shall not live on bread alone, but on every word that proceeds out of the mouth of God." Peter said we should long for the nourishment of the Word with the same craving as a baby longs for the nourishment of milk (1 Pet. 2:2).

127

James 1:21 says, "Putting aside all filthiness and all that remains of wickedness, in humility *receive the word* implanted" (emphasis added). That's our part. We must receive the Word with a pure heart and a humble attitude. As we do, it progressively renews and transforms our thinking, attitudes, actions, and words. It trains us in righteousness.

Regular, concentrated meditation and thoughtful study of God's Word are essential to spiritual health and victory. Even those who know the Bible well must be refreshed by its power and reminded of its truths. That's why Peter said,

> I shall always be ready to remind you of these things, even though you already know them, and have been established in the truth which is present with you. And I consider it right, as long as I am in this earthly [body], to stir you up by way of reminder . . . [so that] after my departure you may be able to call these things to mind. (2 Pet. 1:12–15)

On Paul's departure from Ephesus, he charged the elders there to stay true to the only source of spiritual strength and health: "I commend you to God and to the word of His grace, which is able to build you up and to give you the inheritance among all those who are sanctified" (Acts 20:32).

Paul shared Peter's perspective on the importance of being constantly reminded of what we already know: "Finally, my brethren, rejoice in the Lord. To write the same things again is no trouble to me, and it is a safeguard for you" (Phil. 3:1). We must systematically refresh ourselves not just with new truth, but also with old truths we have already mastered. That kind of intense focus on God's Word assures that we will be "adequate [perfect, complete], equipped for every good work" (2 Tim. 3:17).

An Appeal for Discernment

Many have lost confidence in the sufficiency of God's Word because they have never really learned its truths or how to apply it properly. Yet Scripture is a crucial part of the spiritual armor that makes up the essential equipment for the complete Christian (Eph. 6:11). The sword of the Spirit, God's Word (v. 17), is the only offensive weapon Paul mentions in that passage. Like any weapon, it must be used skillfully to be most effective. That is implied in the Greek word Paul used for "sword." It isn't *rhomphaia*, which refers to a broad sword, but *machaira*, a small dagger. And the Greek term translated "word" is *rhēma*. It speaks of a specific statement. Just as a small dagger is applied with skill and precision to a vital area of the body, so we must use the Word carefully and expertly, applying specific principles from it to every situation we face. That's how Jesus dealt with Satan in Matthew 4:1–11 (see also Luke 4:1–13).

How's your skill with the spiritual sword? Do you have a thorough grasp of Scripture and know how to apply it with precision? If you learn how to use it properly, the Word can be an effective weapon for any challenge. If you waste time and energy with manmade, plastic weapons, however, you'll find yourself a defenseless victim in the spiritual battle.

Luke described the Jewish people at Berea as noble (Acts 17:11) because they searched the Scriptures before they accepted anything Paul said as truth. If only Christians today would be so noble! It is a praiseworthy thing to uphold God's truth and affirm those who accurately proclaim it. On the other hand, it is spiritually lethal to tolerate false doctrine and apostate teachers—and foolish not to know the difference. But the spirit of ignorant tolerance that plagues the church today often brands any attempt to scrutinize others' teaching as narrow-minded, unloving, or divisive. The flip side of tolerance of error is indifference to truth—and that is disastrous.

The church has become lazy. It has moved away from careful biblical thinking and has tolerated far too much shoddy teaching. Fewer and fewer Christians are approaching life with the Berean perspective. They haven't developed the habit of discerning or applying biblical principles to their daily situations. Consequently, when they get into problems, they assume Scripture can't help them. Then they turn to humanistic or worldly alternatives that only compound their grief. They witlessly renounce their sufficiency in Christ and then struggle to fill the void with utterly inadequate substitutes.

Moreover, by failing to build only on biblical principles, they open the door to all kinds of evil influences. Dr. Robert Thomas, professor of New Testament at The Master's Seminary, warns:

> People don't often go heretical all at once. It is gradual. And they do not do so intentionally most of the time. They slip into it through shoddiness and laziness in handling the word of truth. . . . All it takes to start the road to heresy is a craving for something new and different, a flashy new idea, along with a little laziness or carelessness or lack of precision in handling the truth of God.
>
> All around us today are startling reminders of doctrinal slippage and outright failure. In case after case someone who should have known the truth of God better failed in upholding that truth.[3]

And so the church is losing its ability to discern between truth and error. That in turn is reflected in unholy living among those who identify with the church. We're seeing those things happen with alarming suddenness.

Sadly, some of the most careless handlers of Scripture are those whose responsibility it is to teach. The sloppy theology that comes from many contemporary pulpits is shocking. Can the church afford to countenance leaders who approach their calling with a lackadaisical recklessness? Certainly not. Imagine the practical implications if teachers of mathematics or chemistry were as slapdash as some who handle the Word of God. Would you want to be served by a pharmacist, for example, who used the "best guess" method of filling prescriptions? Or would you take your business to an architect who worked mostly with approximations? Or would you allow a surgeon to operate on you with a table knife instead of a scalpel? The sad truth is that society would quickly grind to a halt if most professions approached their work the way many Bible teachers do.

Note what Dr. Thomas writes about the importance of precision in teaching the Bible:

> Precision . . . is a compelling desire to master the truth of God in more definitive terms, to facilitate a more accurate presentation of that truth to others and to safeguard against doctrinal slippage that leads to error and false doctrine. . . . Everyone will not appreciate precision and willingly assent to its importance. We live in a world that would have us to be satisfied, in certain cases, with rough estimate, particularly when it comes to theological matters. It takes a lot of patience and "thick skin" to put up with the criticism and outright opposition that will come when God's servant insists on accuracy. . . .

There are too many "ball-park" interpreters and expositors today. The theological atmosphere of evangelicalism is saturated with a dense fog of uncertainty and misplaced emphases in handling the Word of God. Many churches are on the rocks because of careless hermeneutics, ignorance of biblical languages, and unsystematic theology. Rough estimates as to what this or that passage means will not do. We need qualified expositors who will take the time and make the necessary sacrifices to do their homework well and bring clarity to the minds of God's people as they read and study God's holy Word.[4]

Recently on a Sunday morning as people gathered for worship in a church not far from where I live, the beams holding up the roof began to splinter and collapse. Fortunately no one was injured, but the church building is unusable without total rebuilding. Poor design by the engineers has left that congregation without a meeting place. Sad as it is, the collapse of a building's roof can't come close to the disaster of a spiritual collapse in churches designed by inept "engineers" of the Word. Yet the latter happens far more frequently.

Preach the Word . . . and Nothing but the Word

It is tragic when the builder himself is responsible for flaws that will inevitably cause his structure to collapse, but often that's the case in the church. Apostate and incompetent clergymen abound, and are becoming the norm rather than the exception. In *Preach the Word!*, Robert L. Reymond, professor of systematic theology and apologetics at Covenant Theological Seminary in St. Louis, Missouri, identifies the problem this way:

I say it with sadness, but in my opinion it is true nonetheless that at a time when opportunities for the church of Jesus Christ to make real advances were never better, a theological illiteracy which invites the rise of wholesale heresy pervades the church, traceable both to apostate clergymen and to a distressing lack of theologically articulate spokesmen among evangelicals capable of correcting the maladies that afflict the church.

Do not misunderstand me. There is no paucity of preachers. But the burning question is, how many are really theologically qualified to minister in this day?

He admonishes preachers to:

Covenant with God to learn all that you can from His inscripturated revelation to His church about what men are to believe concerning Him, His Christ, and His great salvation . . . and what duty God requires of them, and to preach what He teaches you to the dear church for whom Christ died, for the improvement of its health and the equipping of His children for those good works which God Himself has decreed for it. And while it will ever be the case that it is He alone who can give the increase, bathe your entire labor for Him in the fervent prayer that you may be used to plant His word and to water it in the souls of needy men.[5]

Evangelical preaching ought to reflect our conviction that God's Word is infallible and inerrant. Too often it does not. In fact, there is a trend in contemporary evangelicalism away from expository, doctrinal preaching and a movement toward an experience-centered, pragmatic, shallow, topical approach in the pulpit.

Churchgoers are seen as consumers who have to be sold something they like. Pastors must preach what people want to hear rather than what God wants proclaimed.

This is the very issue Paul addressed in 2 Timothy 4:3–4: "The time will come when they will not endure sound doctrine; but wanting to have their ears tickled, they will accumulate for themselves teachers in accordance to their own desires; and will turn away their ears from the truth, and will turn aside to myths." Paul forbade Timothy to preach that way.

What does God's Word say about how we are to minister? Jesus said, "Go . . . and make disciples of all the nations, baptizing them in the name of the Father and the Son and the Holy Spirit, teaching them to observe all that I commanded you" (Matt. 28:19–20). Paul said, "Until I come, give attention to the public reading of Scripture, to exhortation and teaching" (1 Tim. 4:13). "And the things which you have heard from me in the presence of many witnesses, these entrust to faithful men, who will be able to teach others also" (2 Tim. 2:2). "As for you, speak the things which are fitting for sound doctrine" (Titus 2:1).

Preaching that does not strive to communicate God's truth to man is not legitimate preaching. The preacher who avoids doctrine because he thinks it is too technical or impractical has abdicated his biblical responsibility. He is called to speak with the authority of God, and no one can do that who is not an expositor of God's Word. Moving stories, moralistic advice, psychology, comedy, and opinion all are void of certainty. Only the authoritative proclamation of the Word fits the intent of God in the call to preach. Those other things are tools for the kind of ear-tickling preaching Paul cautioned Timothy about:

I solemnly charge you in the presence of God and of Christ Jesus, who is to judge the living and the dead, and by His appearing and His kingdom: preach the word; be ready in season and out of season; reprove, rebuke, exhort, with great patience and instruction. For the time will come when they will not endure sound doctrine; but wanting to have their ears tickled, they will accumulate for themselves teachers in accordance to their own desires; and will turn away their ears from the truth, and will turn aside to myths. But you, be sober in all things, endure hardship, do the work of an evangelist, fulfill your ministry. (2 Tim. 4:1–5)

That solemn charge came as the apostle, knowing his death was imminent (vv. 6–9), passed the mantle to his son in the faith. He commanded Timothy to stick with the confrontive preaching of the powerful Word. When he says "be ready" (v. 2), he uses a military term meaning "to be at one's post." Faithfulness to duty is the idea it conveys. It is a call to seize every opportunity "in season and out"— whether convenient or inconvenient, popular or unpopular. There is no closed season on the Word. We are to proclaim it constantly and incessantly.

The tone of such preaching is to "reprove," which has the idea of refuting and deals with the mind; "rebuke" confronts the emotions as sin is exposed; and "exhort" emphasizes the call to repentance and obedience. All that is to be done with great patience through careful instruction.

That is the divine mandate.

It won't be easy, however. Why? Because people won't come to hear, won't tolerate strong preaching of the Word. Many churches today would not tolerate for two Sundays strong, biblical preaching that confronts their doctrinal

135

error, refutes it, lays conviction of sin on the people, or exhorts them to holy obedience. They would replace such a preacher with teachers who feed their desires and tickle their ears. They want something sensational, entertaining, self-benefiting, ego-building—something that feels good and produces a pleasant sensation. For the sake of such a feeling they will gladly exchange the truth for fables, myths, stories.

"Give us what we want!" they cry and tolerate only the preachers who do. A look at a few Old Testament passages reveals this is nothing new. Isaiah ministered in a generation much like ours:

> For this is a rebellious people, false sons,
> Sons who refuse to listen
> To the instruction of the Lord;
> Who say to the seers, "You must not see visions";
> And to the prophets, "You must not prophesy to us
>   what is right,
> Speak to us pleasant words,
> Prophesy illusions." (Isa. 30:9–10)

The Lord Himself told Jeremiah, "The prophets prophesy falsely / And the priests rule on their own authority; / And My people love it so!" (Jer. 5:31). Micah observed poignantly, "If a man walking after wind and falsehood / Had told lies and said, / 'I will speak out to you concerning wine and liquor,' / He would be spokesman to this people" (Micah 2:11).

Throughout its history the church has faced similar periods of apostasy and lack of discernment. In a preface to one of his sermons, Charles H. Spurgeon confronted some of the clergymen of his day with this parable:

136

In the days of Nero there was great shortness of food in the city of Rome, although there was abundance of corn to be purchased at Alexandria. A certain man who owned a vessel went down to the sea coast, and there he noticed many hungry people straining their eyes toward the sea, watching for the vessels that were to come from Alexandria with corn.

When these vessels came to the shore, one by one, the poor people wrung their hands in bitter disappointment, for on board the galleys there was nothing but sand which the tyrant emperor had compelled them to bring for use in the arena. It was infamous cruelty, when men were dying of hunger to command trading vessels to go to and fro, and bring nothing else but sand for gladiatorial shows, when wheat was so greatly needed.

Then the merchant whose vessel was moored by the [wharf] said to his shipmaster, "Take thou good heed that thou bring nothing back with thee from Alexandria but corn; and whereas, aforetime thou hast brought in the vessel a measure or two of sand, bring thou not so much as would lie upon a penny this time. Bring thou nothing else, I say, but wheat; for these people are dying, and now we must keep our vessels for this one business of bringing food for them."

Spurgeon went on to observe:

Alas! I have seen certain mighty galleys of late loaded with nothing but mere sand of philosophy and speculation, and I have said within myself, "Nay, but I will bear nothing in my ship but the revealed truth of God, the bread of life so greatly needed by the people."[6]

That captures my own feelings.

137

7

Religious Hedonism

The word of God is living and active and sharper than any two-edged sword, and piercing as far as the division of soul and spirit, of both joints and marrow, and able to judge the thoughts and intentions of the heart. And there is no creature hidden from His sight, but all things are open and laid bare to the eyes of Him with whom we have to do.

Hebrews 4:12–13

You have been born again not of seed which is perishable but imperishable, that is, through the living and abiding word of God.

1 Peter 1:23

NOT LONG AGO A MAN I HAD NEVER MET BEFORE walked into my office and said, "I need help. I feel strange coming to you, because I'm not even a Christian. I'm Jewish. Until a few weeks ago I had never even been in a church. But I need help from someone, so I decided to talk to you."

I assured him I would do my best to help him. I asked him to sit down and explain what was troubling him. The conversation went something like this:

"I've been divorced twice," he said, "and now I'm living with a woman who is my lover. I don't even like her, but I haven't got the courage to leave her and go back to my second wife.

"I'm a medical doctor," he continued. "Worse, I'm an abortionist. I kill babies for a living. Last year in my clinic we did nine million dollars' worth of abortions. I don't do only therapeutic abortions; I do abortions for any reason. And if a woman doesn't have a reason, I give her a reason.

"Six weeks ago I came to Grace Community Church on a Sunday morning, and I've been coming every week since. Last week you preached a message called, 'Delivered to Satan.' If there was ever anyone on earth who was delivered to Satan, it's me. I know I'm doomed to hell because of what I've done. I'm absolutely miserable and unhappy. I'm continually seeing a psychoanalyst and I'm not getting any help at all. I can't stand the guilt of all this. I don't know what to do about it. Can you help me?"

I said to him, "No. I can't help you."

He looked at me, startled. Sheer desperation was evident in his face.

I let it sink in.

Then I said, "But I know Someone who can help you: Jesus Christ."

He said sadly, "But I don't know who He is. I've been taught all my life not to believe in Him."

I said, "Would you like to know who Jesus Christ is?"

He said, "I would if He can help me."

"Here's what I want you to do." I reached over and took a Bible off my desk and opened it to the Gospel of John. I said, "I want you to take this book home and read this part called the Gospel of John. I want you to keep reading until you know who Jesus Christ is. Then call me again."

Later that week I was recounting the incident for the pastor of another church. He said, "Is that all you gave him? Just the Gospel of John? Why didn't you give him some helps, some tapes, some questions to answer—something? Just the Bible?"

I said, "Don't worry. The Bible is like a lion. You don't need to defend it. Just open the door and let it out. It'll take care of itself. If his heart is open at all, the Bible can do more to reach him than I could do with reams of other study material. What could I possibly give him that's more powerful than Scripture itself?"

The next Friday I received a telephone call. The doctor wanted to see me again. We made an appointment. He showed up precisely on time, came into the office, walked past me as if I weren't there, sat on the couch, dropped the Bible beside him, and said, "I know who He is."

I said, "You do?"

He said, "Yes, I do."

"Who is He?" I asked.

"I'll tell you one thing—He's not just a man."

I said, "Really? Who is He?"

"He's God!" he said with finality.

"You, a Jew, are telling me that Jesus Christ is God?" I asked. "How do you know that?"

He said, "It's clear. It's right there in the Gospel of John."

"What convinced you?" I asked.

"Look at the words He said, and look at the things He did! No one could say and do those things unless He was God." He was echoing the apostle John's thesis perfectly.

I nodded enthusiastically.

He was on a roll. "Do you know what else He did? He rose from the dead! They buried Him, and three days later, He came back from the dead! *That* proves He is God, doesn't it? God Himself came into this world!"

I asked him, "Do you know why He came?"

"Yes. He came to die for my sin."

"How do you know that?" I asked.

"Because I liked John so well I read Romans. And as soon as I clean up my life I'm going to become a Christian."

I said, "That's the wrong approach. Receive Him as your Lord and Savior now, and let *Him* clean up your life." Then I asked the man, "What would such a decision mean in your career?"

"Well," he said, "I spent this afternoon writing my resignation letter to the abortion clinic. When I get out of here I'm going to call my second wife and bring her to church with me." And he did.

Why would anyone question Scripture's power to reach such a person? The fact is, nothing I could have ever said to that man would have been more effective than the Spirit-inspired truth of the Bible itself in convicting him of his sin and illuminating his need for Christ. As Hebrews 4:12 says, "The word of God is living and active and sharper than any two-edged sword, and piercing as far as the division of soul and spirit, of both joints and marrow, and able to judge the thoughts and intentions of the heart." The Word of God is perfectly able to open an unbeliever's eyes to the truth of the gospel, convict him of sin—or even do radical surgery on his soul.

Yet there are many today who believe the truth of God's Word isn't enough to move people to repentance. Some believe we must also be able to exhibit signs, wonders, and resurrections to convince unbelievers of the truth of the Word. Others feel we must disguise the gospel in a cloak of subtlety, make it culturally relevant, or otherwise adapt it to accommodate unbelievers' hardness of heart. They would rather operate with synthetic seed than sow the living seed of God's Word. Both perspectives deny the inherent power of God's Word and Spirit, as well as the place of His sovereignty in redemption.

I'm amazed by what people believe they must do to augment the power of God's Word. I read an article about a well-known gospel singer who has been criticized for dressing provocatively and sunbathing in the nude. Her pastor, wanting to defend her, said she was only trying to use sexuality "in a godly sense" in order to reach her culture. Does God need a sexy singer to do what the Bible doesn't have the power to do? That man's comment reflects what many in the church today seem to believe: you must have an angle to present the gospel to a hostile world. You must be indirect, and winsome, and simplistic, and careful not to turn anyone off. And if—God forbid—someone should be offended or reject the message, it means you have failed. Is that a biblical perspective?

No, it is not. It has opened the door to some bizarre evangelistic strategies. The church apes nearly every fad of secular society. Heavy-metal rock, rap, graffiti, break dancing, body building, brick smashing, jazzercize, interpretive dance, and stand-up comedy all have been added to the evangelical repertoire. Turn on most Christian television stations, and you'll see a parade of talk shows, music videos, carnival acts, comedy routines, musical variety shows, and other performances virtually identical to the programming on secular stations except that the Christian stations use the name of Jesus. It is nothing but hedonism under the guise of religion.

Many assume that without some gimmick, the gospel message just won't reach people, and unless we accommodate it to the fashion of our day, we can't hope for it to be effective. Lamentably, unholy living on the part of shallow professors of Christ has rendered the church's testimony impotent. Thus modern churches feel they must plan and program for attracting unbelievers who cannot be persuaded with revealed truth—because those same people have been repelled by the hypocrisy of church members' unholy living.

Liberalism's Legacy

The notion that Scripture itself is inadequate for evangelism is certainly not new. Nor is the strategy of trying to update the gospel message by using the fashion of the day to make it more appealing. A 1928 article by the infamous Harry Emerson Fosdick argued bitterly that expository preaching is inherently irrelevant:

> Within a paragraph or two after a sermon has started, wide areas of any congregation ought to begin recognizing that the preacher is tackling something of vital concern to them. . . . And if any preacher is not doing this, even though he have at his disposal both erudition and oratory, he is not functioning at all.
>
> Many preachers, for example, indulge habitually in what they call expository sermons. They take a passage from Scripture and, proceeding on the assumption that the people attending church that morning are deeply concerned about what the passage means, they spend their half hour or more on historical exposition of the verse or chapter, ending with some appended practical application to the auditors. Could any procedure be more surely predestined to dullness and futility? Who seriously supposes that, as a matter of fact, one in a hundred of the congregation cares, to start with, what

Moses, Isaiah, Paul, or John meant in those special verses, or came to church deeply concerned about it? Nobody who talks to the public so assumes that the vital interests of the people are located in the meaning of words spoken two thousand years ago. . . .

Preachers who pick out texts from the Bible and then proceed to give their historic settings, their logical meaning in the context, their place in the theology of the writer, with a few practical reflections appended, are grossly misusing the Bible.[1]

Fosdick, of course, was a noted infidel who rejected Scripture altogether. His philosophy was that the preacher must never start from Scripture and preach to his people; rather he should start with his people's interests and felt needs, and then reason his way to some supposed solution of their perceived problems. If Scripture could be used for illustrative purposes, fine, but it was never to be the starting point:

The modern preacher . . . should clearly visualize some real need, perplexity, sin, or desire in his auditors, and then should throw on the problem all the light he can find in the Scripture or anywhere else. No matter what one's theory about the Bible is, this is the effective approach to preaching. The Bible is a searchlight, not so much intended to be looked at as to be thrown upon a shadowed spot.[2]

Fosdick continued:

There is nothing that people are so interested in as themselves, their own problems, and the way to solve them. That fact is basic. No preaching that neglects it can raise a ripple on a congregation.[3]

Ironically, that liberal, humanistic approach to preaching is precisely the route many who call themselves evangelical are taking today. The pastor of one large church echoes Fosdick's philosophy: "We have put a lot of time and thought into what non-churched people want from a Sunday morning service, and we have concluded that they basically want four things: Anonymity, uncomplicated teaching, a non-threatening environment, and contemporary relevancy."

His church is doing its best to offer what the unchurched say they are looking for. The quest for relevancy has led this church and others like it to kick aside virtually every conventional expression of worship. Sunday services are first-class musical-comedy-drama productions—no Bible teaching or expository preaching. The offertory is more likely to be the theme from *Rocky* than music with a spiritual message. Everything possible is done to cater to the appetites of the unchurched. Nothing is permitted that would challenge them or make them uncomfortable. The approach has proved so successful in drawing crowds that hundreds, perhaps thousands, of churches nationwide have now adopted the same philosophy.

Those churches have turned to merchandising schemes and entertainment media in an effort to appeal to people. Simply preaching the Word is out. That's too confrontive, and the unvarnished gospel is too offensive. Bible exposition is deemed distasteful. Better to charm people first, then slip the gospel in subtly. Churches that have bought this misguided philosophy believe they must provide entertainment and good feelings rather than profound truth and deep experiences of worship, prayer, and conviction.

Any pastor who follows that pattern and fails to preach the Word is prostituting the ministry. And any church that aims to entertain the unconverted has placed itself in opposition to God. "Whoever wishes to be a friend of the world makes himself an enemy of God" (James 4:4). The church is supposed to confront the world. The message God has called us to preach is not designed to make sinners comfortable. The *fear of God* is what should motivate us to persuade men (2 Cor. 5:10–11). Many preachers today are fearful only of offending people; hence they preach an insipid, powerless message that is in fact an offense to God.

Contrast that trend with what we know of preaching in the early church. Paul challenged the Galatian church, saying, "Am I now seeking the favor of men, or of God? Or am I striving to please men? If I were still trying to please men, I would not be a bond-servant of Christ" (Gal. 1:10). He wrote, "I am not ashamed of the gospel" (Rom. 1:16).

The way Paul confronted Felix and Drusilla (Acts 24:24–27) further defies some of the cardinal axioms of the shameful evangelism of our day. He declared God's truth to them without regard to their status, position, power, or prestige ("Therefore . . . we recognize no man according to the flesh," 2 Cor. 5:16). He offered them no words of comfort, consolation, or encouragement; in fact, his message frightened Felix so much that Felix sent Paul away (v. 25). The apostle discussed three matters with Felix and Drusilla: "righteousness, self-control and the judgment to come" (v. 25). Those, of course, are the very focus of the Holy Spirit's convicting ministry (John 16:8–11). And they would have been particularly alarming topics for Felix and Drusilla, whose debauchery was legendary throughout the Roman Empire. That did not dissuade Paul from boldly challenging them.

Remember, too, that Paul was appearing before Felix as a prisoner before a judge. Felix could have ordered Paul's release from prison. Still, the apostle did not attempt to mollycoddle or flatter him. Paul's only concern was preaching the truth to this man, whom he viewed as a sinner in need of salvation. He preferred leaving him miserable and terrified knowing his need of a Savior rather than making him comfortable—though ignorantly on his way to hell.

When Peter preached at Pentecost, people were cut to the heart (Acts 2:37–41). He didn't undertake to win them over. He didn't try to charm them, entertain them, or make them feel good. He made no effort to engineer a positive response; he just proclaimed the truth. That's the only methodology the Holy Spirit uses. Those who employ any other technique are operating on their own.

A single-minded commitment to glorifying God characterized every facet of ministry in the New Testament church. Those Christians were not nearly as concerned with the world's opinion as churches today seem to be. When believers met on the first day of the week, it was not to be entertained or to amuse their pagan neighbors. Teaching, fellowship, the breaking of bread, and prayer (Acts 2:42) constituted their complete program. Everything revolved around the preaching of the Word (2 Tim. 2:2). On at least one occasion in the church at Troas, the apostle Paul expounded God's Word until after midnight (Acts 20:7)—then stayed until daybreak talking with the people (v. 11). Most churches today would be up in arms if the preacher proclaimed God's truth for that long!

Worship services in many churches today are like a merry-go-round. You drop a token in the collection box; it's good for a ride. There's music and lots of motion up and down. The ride is carefully timed and seldom varies in length. Lots of good feelings are generated, and it is the one ride you can be sure will never be the least bit threatening or challenging. But though you spend the whole time feeling as if you're moving forward, you get off exactly where you got on.

There is seemingly no limit to what some churches will do to entertain people. I know of churches that now offer musical extravaganzas that include dancing and secular rock music, exhibitions virtually indistinguishable from Las Vegas shows. One pastor, when asked why he allowed such a performance at his church, said, "It attracts people." That's a pragmatic approach to ministry—whatever works is thought to be acceptable.

What's Wrong with Pragmatism?

The error of pragmatism is that it regards methodologies that "work" as more important and more viable than those that are biblical. A pragmatist is concerned primarily with whether a given practice is expedient, not necessarily with whether it is in harmony with Scripture. He starts with the question, "What do the unchurched want?" and builds his strategy from there, rather than asking the question, "What does Scripture teach about church ministry?" and following a biblical pattern.

The contemporary trend of pragmatism utterly ignores the biblical priorities for the church. Church meetings are not supposed to be designed for unbelievers. According to Scripture, the church comes together for worship, fellowship, edification, and mutual encouragement within the body (Acts 20:7ff; 1 Cor. 16:1–2; Heb. 10:24–25). The preaching of God's Word is to be the essential focal point for all corporate worship and ministry (1 Tim. 6:2; 2 Tim. 4:2). The emphasis should be prayerful, adoring communion with God, not entertainment or any expression of self-indulgence (1 Cor. 11:17–22). In short, the activities outlined in Acts 2:42 are the only valid business of the church: "the apostles' teaching . . . fellowship . . . the breaking of bread and . . . prayer."

Furthermore, pragmatism attacks the sufficiency of God's Word in evangelism. We don't need to market the gospel, disguise it, tone it down, or otherwise try to make it acceptable to unbelievers. The plain gospel is the power of God unto salvation.

Wherever pragmatism exists in the church, there is always a corresponding de-emphasis on Christ's sufficiency, God's sovereignty, biblical integrity, the power of prayer, and Spirit-led ministries. The result is a man-centered ministry that attempts to accomplish divine purposes by superficial programs and human methodology rather than by the Word or the power of the Spirit.

Pragmatism's ally is arminianism, the theology that denies God's sovereign election and affirms that man must decide on his own to trust or reject Christ. That places on the evangelist the burden of using technique that is clever enough, imaginative enough, or convincing enough to sway a person's decision. The *content* of the message is thus subjugated to the issue of how it is packaged.

I don't deny the importance of powerful, persuasive preaching and teaching. Paul himself was a brilliant communicator (for example, see Acts 18:4; 19:26; 26:28–29; 28:23). But to teach or imply that human technique can bring someone to Christ is contrary to Scripture (John 6:37, 44), and in effect denies God's sovereign grace. Apart from Christ and the ministry of His Spirit we can accomplish nothing (John 15:5; 2 Cor. 10:4).

Those who substitute entertainment for a clear proclamation of the truth are in conflict with God's design for the church. Although they believe external results justify their methods, they are doing more harm than good—no matter how large the crowds they draw. Methodology used simply to excite an otherwise indifferent society is a poor substitute for the clear teaching of Scripture. A few months of strong, straightforward, no-frills preaching on repentance and holiness would reduce the attendance at those churches, but it would also reveal who is genuinely redeemed or being led by the Holy Spirit to redemption.

Nevertheless, pragmatism is reshaping virtually every facet of evangelical ministry. Where preaching can still be found, it tends to be man-centered and dominated by a relational mentality that attempts to reconcile man to men, not man to God. Its often unstated but real goal is to salve people who are totally immersed in themselves, *their* hurts, and *their* perceived needs. Thus it is fueled by and further inflames society's bent toward selfishness.

Robert Schuller sketched a pragmatist's manifesto almost a decade ago:

> For the church to address the unchurched with a theocentric attitude is to invite failure in mission. The nonchurched who have no vital belief in a relationship with God will spurn, reject, or simply ignore the theologian, church spokesperson, preacher, or missionary who approaches with Bible in hand, theology

on the brain and the lips, and expects nonreligious persons to suspend their doubts and swallow the theocentric assertions as fact. The unconverted will, I submit, take notice when I demonstrate genuine concern about their needs and honestly care about their human hurts.

For decades now we have watched the church in Western Europe and in America decline in power, membership, and influence. I believe that this decline is the result of our placing theocentric communications above the meeting of the deeper emotional and spiritual needs of humanity.[4]

That is an overt appeal for the church to proclaim a man-centered, not a God-centered, message. He believes the basic defect in modern Christianity is "the failure to proclaim the gospel in a way that can satisfy every person's deepest need—one's spiritual hunger for glory."[5] He couldn't be more wrong. The gospel is about God's glory, not man's.

Rarely are the goals of pragmatism stated so plainly. Clearly those views are antithetical to God's Word. Yet many who give verbal assent to the truth of Scripture have bought the notion that we must somehow adapt the biblical message to make it fit with people's perceived needs.

The most basic truths of our faith have fallen victim to this self-centered theology. Many modern-day evangelists have reduced the gospel message to little more than a formula by which people can live a happy and more fulfilling life. Sin is now defined by how it affects man, not how it dishonors God. Salvation is often presented as a means of receiving what Christ offers without obeying what He commands. The focus has shifted from God's glory to man's benefit. The gospel of persevering faith has given way to a kind of religious hedonism. Jesus, contemporary theology implies, is your ticket to avoiding all of life's pains and experiencing all of life's pleasures.

Thus has pragmatism succumbed to the humanistic notion that man exists for his own satisfaction. Humanism teaches that people must have all their perceived needs and desires met if they are to be happy. To accommodate that view, pragmatism concocts a gospel message that sounds like a guarantee of fulfilled wishes rather than a call to repentance, forgiveness, and reconciliation with God. Many who call themselves Christians have even abandoned the gospel altogether and instead call people to pursue self-esteem; political influence; economic equality; security and significance; prosperity; health, wealth, and happiness; or any number of similarly self-serving aspirations. Rarely is the gospel presented well enough for unrepentant sinners to reject it.

Walter Chantry correctly addressed the problem in his book *Today's Gospel: Authentic or Synthetic?*:

> Much of modern preaching is anaemic, with the life-blood of God's nature absent from the message. Evangelists centre their message upon man. Man has sinned and missed a great blessing. If man wants to retrieve his immense loss he must act thus and so. But the Gospel of Christ is very different. It begins with God and His glory. It tells men that they have offended a holy God, who will by no means pass by sin. It reminds sinners that the only hope of salvation is to be found in the grace and power of this same God. Christ's Gospel sends men to beg pardon of the Holy One.
>
> There is a wide difference between these two messages. The one seeks to blaze a trail to Heaven for man while

155

ignoring the Lord of Glory. The other labours to magnify the God of all grace in the salvation of men.[6]

Evangelism that focuses only on the promise of fulfilled needs is a deadly corruption of the biblical message. In his insightful biography of the late D. Martyn Lloyd-Jones, Iain Murray accurately observes,

> An evangelist must exercise care lest by a mere appeal to self-interest he induces a "decision" which, far from being saving, is perfectly consistent with a person remaining in an unregenerate condition. A presentation of the gospel chiefly in terms of its ability to fulfil man's need of happiness and other blessings, and which fails to show that man's wrong relationship to God "is much worse than everything else" in his condition, may well receive a considerable though temporary success. A salvation conceived "not as something primarily that brings us to God but as something that gives *us* something" requires no real conviction of sin in order to its acceptance. ML–J was not surprised that such evangelism could be carried on with glibness and lightness and that its result was to add the unspiritual and the careless to the churches. The true convert always wants deliverance from the power as well as the guilt of sin.[7]

The "needs" mentality has not only corrupted the gospel, but it has also distorted the doctrine of sanctification. Many Christians think they can't be effective for the Lord until all their problems are solved and they have attained personal fulfillment. They see sanctification as the process by which that occurs. In his book *Need: The New Religion*, Tony Walter comments:

It is fashionable to follow the view of some psychologists that the self is a bundle of needs and that personal growth is the business of progressively meeting these needs. Many Christians go along with such beliefs. . . . One mark of the almost total success of this new morality is that the Christian church, traditionally keen on mortifying the desires of the flesh, on crucifying the needs of the self in pursuit of Christ's likeness, has eagerly adopted the language of needs for itself. We now hear that Jesus will meet your every need, as though He were some kind of Divine psychiatrist or Divine detergent and as though God were simply to serve us.[8]

It's not difficult to find evidence of that kind of thinking in the church. Some contemporary ministries flatly admit that satisfying people's perceived needs is their chief goal.

But that's diametrically opposed to what Scripture teaches. The goal of sanctification is to be conformed to Christ's image (Rom. 8:29), not to be self-satisfied. True sanctification is not a matter of assessing yourself and meeting your felt needs. It's a matter of knowing Christ deeply. The more you focus on yourself, the more distracted you will be from the proper path. The more you know Him and commune with Him, the more the Spirit will make you like Him. The more you are like Him, the better you will understand His utter sufficiency for all of life's difficulties. And that is the only way to know *real* satisfaction.

Pragmatism has also created apathy about prayer. That's because the primary motivator of prayer is a sense of dependency on God (for example, see James 4:14–15). Pragmatism, however, creates a false sense of independence and self-sufficiency. It is difficult to force yourself to pray if you think you have a human solution to every problem and a natural resource for every need. The problem is compounded in our society because most of us have more material goods than we need, and we've developed means to deal with whatever other needs might arise. There are "Christian" programs for people who want to improve their looks, physical fitness, self-esteem, investment portfolio, or whatever else might be deficient. Christians who want to have it all here and now can pursue the good life with a vengeance—and feel good about it.

And so, many contemporary Christians are engrossed in a mad quest for instant gratification, obsessed with earthly comfort, and shackled to this present world. I remember a time when the focus was on future hope and people wanted to hear a message about heaven, prophecy, or eschatology. Those are not popular topics today because our minds are set on the present, not the future. Unlike the Thessalonian believers, who longed for Christ's return and for the glories of heaven (1 Thess. 1:9–10), many of us have settled into this life quite comfortably. When a believer dies, some Christians go into fits of despair and depression as if the person went to a worse place, or as if God has taken from us what we so desperately needed in human companionship. We ought rather to rejoice in the assurance that our loved one is in the presence of the Lord, momentarily separated from us but destined for a glad reunion in eternal glory.

The future glories of heaven have been overshadowed by the present glitter of earth, and many Christians have sunk into a health-wealth-and-prosperity comfort zone from which only death itself or the rapture of the church would dare remove them—and even those would be unwelcome intrusions to some. Few people long for heaven.

Perhaps the fatal flaw of pragmatism is that it fails to account properly for human depravity. Man is a fallen creature, and his depravity is so deep and pervasive that he cannot do anything for himself spiritually (Rom. 3:10–11). Therefore the use of human means to accomplish spiritual goals will inevitably fail. That is precisely why God demands that Christians submit to His sovereign rule, learn the principles of spiritual life revealed in the Word, and appropriate the abundant spiritual resources He makes available in Christ (Col. 1:9–15). Those resources are sufficient, entirely apart from human ingenuity, to accomplish God's intended purposes.

"All Things to All Men"

Some have imagined a pragmatic philosophy in the apostle Paul's words in 1 Corinthians 9:20–23:

> To the Jews I became as a Jew, that I might win Jews; to those who are under the Law, as under the Law, though not being myself under the Law, that I might win those who are under the Law; to those who are without law, as without law, though not being without the law of God but under the law of Christ, that I might win those who are without law. To the weak I became weak, that I might win the weak; I have become all things to all men, that I may by all means save some. And I do all things for the sake of the gospel, that I may become a fellow partaker of it.

Paul was speaking of his passion to win the lost at any cost—even extreme personal sacrifice. Verse 19, which launches that section, says, "Though I am free from all men,

I have made myself a slave to all, that I might win the more." He was not advocating that we tailor the message to remove the offense of the cross (Gal. 5:11). Nor would Paul have endorsed the current drive to replace strong preaching with music, drama, and other non-confrontive, non-threatening amusements. In this same epistle to the Corinthians he wrote, "Since in the wisdom of God the world through its wisdom did not come to know God, God was well-pleased through the foolishness of the message preached to save those who believe" (1:21).

That's the opposite of the trend today, with worldly wisdom and carnal diversions replacing the proclamation of God's Word as means of evangelism.

Paul reminded the Corinthians of the example he had been to them: "When I came to you, brethren, I did not come with superiority of speech or of wisdom, proclaiming to you the testimony of God. For I determined to know nothing among you except Jesus Christ, and Him crucified" (1 Cor. 2:1–2). He kept his message simple, straightforward, and direct, letting God's Word pierce their hearts rather than trying to convince them with cleverness or showmanship.

Paul did not want his style of speaking, his personal behavior, his social manners, or any other external issues to be a stumbling block to anyone he was ministering to. He avoided at all cost giving any unnecessary offense; that is, he became "all things to all men" (9:22).

But one thing Paul would never have done to avoid offense was soften or alter the gospel message itself. In fact, his harshest words were a curse pronounced on anyone who would modify the gospel in such a way (Gal. 1:8). He recognized that the message of the cross itself is an enormous stumbling block to unbelievers (Gal. 5:11; Rom. 9:32–33;

1 Cor. 1:23), and he did not shy away from proclaiming it boldly (Acts 19:8; Eph. 6:20). He explicitly condemned ear-tickling preachers (2 Tim. 4:3–5). So it is certain that he would not have entertained for a moment the suggestion that the gospel message could be adapted to appeal to people's selfish or carnal inclinations. Nor would he have tolerated those who feel they must overcome people's resistance and unbelief by repackaging the gospel or by omitting its more difficult demands. He knew such an approach would produce many false converts. That's what led me to this conclusion in my commentary on 1 Corinthians:

> In summary, Paul . . . did not compromise the gospel. He would not change the least truth in the least way in order to satisfy anyone. But he would condescend in any way for anyone if that would in any way help bring him to Christ. He would never set aside a truth of the gospel, but he would gladly restrict his liberty in the gospel. He would not offend Jew, Gentile, or those weak in understanding.
>
> If a person is offended by God's Word, that is his problem. If he is offended by biblical doctrine, standards, or church discipline, that is his problem. That person is offended by God. But if he is offended by our unnecessary behavior or practices—no matter how good and acceptable those may be in themselves—his problem becomes our problem. It is not a problem of law but a problem of love, and love always demands more than the law. "Whoever slaps you on your right cheek, turn to him the other also. And if anyone wants to sue you, and take your shirt, let him have your coat also. And whoever shall force you to go one mile, go with him two." (Matt. 5:39–41)

Paul's life centered in living out the gospel and in preaching and teaching the gospel. Nothing else was of any concern to him. I do all things for the sake of the gospel. His life was the gospel. He therefore set aside anything that would hinder its power and effectiveness.[9]

"The Power of God for Salvation"

Paul was certain that God's Word itself was sufficient to provoke true saving faith in the hardest unbelievers' hearts. He wrote, "I am not ashamed of the gospel, for it is the power of God for salvation to everyone who believes" (Rom. 1:16). Unfortunately, many evangelicals have moved away from that confidence in recent years.

Jesus also gave testimony to the perfect sufficiency of Scripture in Luke 16:19–31. There He tells the story of a rich man and a poor beggar named Lazarus. Both had died. In the afterlife, the rich man found himself in Hades. He wanted Lazarus, who was in heaven, to go back and warn his brothers about the torments of an eternity without God. He made the same mistake that many people today make: he assumed that something unusual would convince unbelievers to be saved. But if people reject God's Word, they'll reject a miracle. Abraham told the rich man, "They have Moses and the Prophets; let them hear them" (v. 29). The rich man, sure that his brothers needed something more than Scripture, pleaded, "No, Father Abraham, but if someone goes to them from the dead, they will repent!" (v. 30). Abraham's answer forever affirms the utter sufficiency of Scripture for every evangelistic endeavor: "He said to him, 'If they do not listen to Moses and the Prophets, neither will they be persuaded if someone rises from the dead'" (v. 31).

Jesus Himself said, "He who hears My word, and believes Him who sent Me, has eternal life, and does not come into judgment, but has passed out of death into life" (John 5:24). The essence of the gospel is hearing Christ's Word and believing in God.

In the parable of the sower (Luke 8:5–15), Jesus likened God's Word to a seed, which when planted in fertile soil (a receptive heart) produces new life and much spiritual fruit.

Jesus also said, "I did not speak on My own initiative, but the Father Himself who sent Me has given Me commandment, what to say, and what to speak. And I know that His commandment is eternal life; therefore the things I speak, I speak just as the Father has told Me" (John 12:49–50). He knew the saving power of God's Word; so He spoke only what the Father instructed Him to speak.

The apostle John said, "These [things] have been written that you may believe that Jesus is the Christ, the Son of God; and that believing you may have life in His name" (John 20:31). Believing God's Word results in eternal life.

In Romans 10:17 Paul said, "Faith comes from hearing, and hearing by the Word of Christ." Faith comes from hearing the message about Christ. That's why we must faithfully proclaim the gospel to unbelievers. In verses 13–15 He says, "Whoever will call upon the name of the Lord will be saved. How then shall they call upon Him in whom they have not believed? And how shall they believe in Him whom they have not heard? And how shall they hear without a preacher? And how shall they preach unless they are sent?" Sinners need the Word of Christ, which is the source of salvation.

Elsewhere Paul used marriage to illustrate the saving and cleansing work of the Word: "Husbands, love your wives, just as Christ also loved the church and gave Himself up for her; that He might sanctify her, having cleansed her by the washing of water with the word" (Eph. 5:25–26).

James tells us the Father "brought us forth by the word of truth" (James 1:18). "Brought us forth" in that context means "to beget," "redeem," or "save." God saved us by the Word of truth.

First Peter 1:23–25 says,

> You have been born again not of seed which is perishable but imperishable, that is, through the living and abiding word of God. For,
>
> > "All flesh is like grass,
> > And all its glory like the flower of grass.
> > The grass withers,
> > And the flower falls off,
> > But the word of the Lord abides forever."
>
> And this is the word which was preached to you.

Peter affirmed what Jesus taught in the parable of the sower: God's Word is the seed that produces salvation.

Since Scripture imparts salvation, effective evangelism depends on the faithful proclamation of the Word. God will prepare the soil and bring forth the fruit. We must be faithful to plant the seed.

Lydia is a good example of how that works: "A certain woman named Lydia, from the city of Thyatira, a seller of purple fabrics, a worshiper of God, was listening [as Paul preached]; and the Lord opened her heart to respond to the things spoken by [him]" (Acts 16:14). Paul proclaimed Christ, and God opened her heart to receive his words.

How's Your Spiritual Diet?

Overindulgence is a hallmark of our society. Sadly, that's true of the church as well. Many Christians are so stuffed with spiritual junk food that they've lost their appetite for sound biblical teaching. On the other extreme are those who feast on the Word but don't apply it, so they suffer from chronic spiritual lethargy and impotence.

How about you? Are you a man or woman of the Word? No matter where you are in your spiritual growth, Scripture is sufficient to equip you for every good work (2 Tim. 3:17). If you're a Christian who isn't yet grounded in sound doctrine, you need the Word for training and spiritual growth. If you're giving place to sin in your life, you need the reproving and correcting work of the Word.

If you're not a Christian, you need the Word for salvation. Do what my doctor friend did: read the New Testament until you know who Jesus is and what it means to be saved (as you might guess, I suggest starting with the Gospel of John). Confess your sin and ask God to forgive you and to cleanse your heart. That's where it starts. Then you will have all the spiritual resources you need to live a godly life.

My prayer is that you will have an insatiable appetite for sound doctrine and holy living—that you will understand and trust in the inexhaustible sufficiency of our Lord's perfect Word.

8

The Quest for Something More

He is before all things, and in Him all things hold together. He is also head of the body, the church; and He is the beginning, the first-born from the dead; so that He Himself might come to have first place in everything.

Colossians 1:17–18

For in Him all the fulness of Deity dwells in bodily form, and in Him you have been made complete.

Colossians 2:9–10

A STORY IS TOLD ABOUT WILLIAM RANDOLPH Hearst, the late newspaper publisher. Hearst invested a fortune in collecting great works of art. One day he read about some valuable pieces of art and decided that he must add them to his collection. He sent his agent abroad to locate and purchase them. Months went by before the agent returned and reported to Hearst that the items had at last been found—they were stored in his own warehouse. Hearst had purchased them years before!

That is analogous to the alarming number of Christians today who are on a desperate search for spiritual resources they already possess. Theirs is a futile quest for something more. It's a heretical fire fanned in part by the false notion that salvation is insufficient to transform believers and equip them for Christian living. Those thus influenced believe they need something more—more of Christ, more of the Holy Spirit, some kind of ecstatic experience, mysti-cal visions, signs, wonders, miracles, a second blessing, tongues, a higher or deeper spiritual level, or whatever.

But as we have been seeing, to have Jesus is to have every spiritual resource. All we need is found in Him. Rather than attempting to add something to Christ we must simply learn to use the resources that are already ours in Him.

Perhaps the watershed passage in all of Scripture on our sufficiency in Christ is the book of Colossians. Paul wrote it to believers who were strong in faith and love (Col. 1:4) but confused by a heresy that denied Christ's sufficiency. Our study demands a very careful look at some key por-tions of this critical text.

We don't know the precise nature of the heresy in Colosse because Paul didn't define it in detail or spend time naming and denouncing its leaders. Instead he refuted it generally by showing that it was rooted in an inadequate and erroneous view of the Person and work of Christ. He wrote the Colossian church an entire epistle focusing on Christ—His place in the universe, His work in salvation, His preeminence as God, His position as head of the church, and His utter sufficiency for every human need. In so doing, Paul demonstrated that the best defense against false teaching is a thoroughly biblical Christology. He warned the Colossians that attempting to add to or take away from Christ always ends in spiritual disaster.

In chapter 1 Paul writes:

[God has] delivered us from the domain of darkness, and transferred us to the kingdom of His beloved Son, in whom we have redemption, the forgiveness of sins.

And He is the image of the invisible God, the first-born of all creation. For by Him all things were created, both in the heavens and on earth, visible and invisible, whether thrones or dominions or rulers or authorities—all things have been created by Him and for Him.

And He is before all things, and in Him all things hold together. He is also head of the body, the church; and He is the beginning, the first-born from the dead; so that He Himself might come to have first place in everything.

For it was the Father's good pleasure for all the fulness to dwell in Him, and through Him to reconcile all things to Himself, having made peace through the blood of His cross. (vv. 13–20)

The apostle makes a profound summation when he says that in Christ are hidden all the treasures of wisdom and knowledge (2:3) because in Him dwells all the fullness of deity in bodily form. He is head over all rule and authority (2:9–10). He is life itself (3:4)! What more could the apostle say to affirm our Lord's utter sufficiency?

The error he was addressing was multifaceted. It seems clearly to have been an early form of gnosticism (see chapter 1). These Colossian heretics claimed that Christ alone could not elevate someone to the highest spiritual level. They were advocating a variety of artificial spiritual additives, including philosophy (2:8–10), legalism (2:11–17), mysticism (2:18–19), and asceticism (2:20–23).

Christ Plus Philosophy

Our English word "philosophy" is a transliteration of the Greek word *philosophia*, which is a compound of two common Greek words: *phileō* ("to love") and *sophia* ("wisdom"). It literally means "the love of human wisdom." In its broad sense it is man's attempt to explain the nature of the universe including the phenomena of existence, thought, ethics, behavior, aesthetics, and so on.

In Paul's time "everything that had to do with theories about God and the world and the meaning of human life was called 'philosophy' . . . not only in the pagan schools but also in the Jewish schools of the Greek cities."[1] The first-century Jewish historian Josephus adds that there were three forms of philosophies among the Jews: the Pharisees, the Sadducees, and the Essenes.[2]

Paul strongly condemned any philosophical theory about God that professed to show the cause of the world's existence and to offer moral direction apart from divine revelation. In Colossians 2:8–10 he says:

> See to it that no one takes you captive through philosophy[, even] empty deception, according to the tradition of man, according to the elementary principles of the world, rather than according to Christ. For in Him all the fulness of Deity dwells in bodily form, and in Him you have been made complete, and He is the head over all rule and authority.

The phrase "takes you captive" (v. 8) comes from the Greek word *sulagōgeō*, which referred to carrying off captives or other spoils of war. In that sense it conveyed the idea of a kidnapping. It pictures the way the Christ-plus-philosophy heresy was abducting the Colossians away from truth into the slavery of error. Thus the apostle portrayed philosophy as a predator that seeks to enslave undiscerning Christians in "vain deceit" (v. 8, KJV).

"Vain" speaks of something empty, devoid of truth, futile, fruitless, and without effect. Philosophy claims to be true but is utterly deceitful, like a fisherman who captures his unwitting prey by concealing a deadly hook within a tasty morsel of food. The fish thinks it's getting a meal but becomes one instead. Similarly, those who embrace a human philosophy about God or man might think they're getting truth, but instead they get empty deception, which can lead to eternal damnation.

Philosophy is useless because it's grounded in "the tradition of men" and "the elementary principles of the world" (v. 8) rather than in Christ. "The tradition of men" refers to human speculations passed on from generation to generation. Most philosophers stack their teachings on the pile of their predecessors' teachings. One will develop a thought so far, then another develops it further, and on it goes. It's a series of variations within the flow of human tradition that only perpetuates error and compounds ignorance.

The phrase "elementary principles of the world" literally means "things in a column" or "things in a row" (such as 1, 2, 3, or A, B, C). It refers to the kind of instruction one would give a child. Paul was saying that though it purports to be sophisticated, human philosophy is actually rudimentary—childish and unrefined. To abandon biblical revelation for philosophy is like returning to kindergarten after graduating from a university. Even the finest of human philosophy can offer nothing to augment the truth of Christ. It hinders and retards true wisdom and produces only infantile foolishness, error, and deceit.

In 1 Corinthians 1:18–21 Paul says:

> The message of the cross is foolishness to those who are perishing, but to us who are being saved it is the power of God. For it is written:
>
> "I will destroy the wisdom of the wise;
> the intelligence of the intelligent I will frustrate."

Where is the wise man? Where is the scholar? Where is the philosopher of this age? Has not God made foolish the wisdom of the world? For since in the wisdom of God the world through its wisdom did not know him, God was pleased through the foolishness of what was preached to save those who believe. (NIV)

Human wisdom cannot enhance God's revelation. In fact, it inevitably resists and contradicts divine truth. Even the best of human wisdom is mere foolishness in comparison with God's infinite wisdom.

Christians needn't look to human wisdom anyway. They possess the mind of Christ (1 Cor. 2:16). His great, perfect, incomprehensible wisdom is revealed to us in God's Word and through His Spirit. That should stir our hearts to declare with the psalmist:

O how I love Thy law!
It is my meditation all the day.
Thy commandments make me wiser than my enemies,
For they are ever mine.
I have more insight than all my teachers,
For Thy testimonies are my meditation.
I understand more than the aged,
Because I have observed Thy precepts.

I have restrained my feet from every evil way,
That I may keep Thy word.
I have not turned aside from Thine ordinances,
For Thou Thyself hast taught me.

How sweet are Thy words to my taste!
Yes, sweeter than honey to my mouth!

From Thy precepts I get understanding;
Therefore I hate every false way. (Ps. 119:97–104)

Why be held captive to philosophy when you can ascend to God's perfect truth?

In Colossians 2:9–10 Paul draws a significant parallel: "In [Christ] all the fulness of Deity dwells in bodily form, and in Him you have been made complete." "Fullness" and "complete" in that passage are translations of the same Greek word (*plērōma*). Just as Christ is utterly divine, so we are utterly sufficient in Him. Human wisdom adds nothing to what is already revealed in Christ.

Our sufficiency in Christ is grounded on complete salvation and complete forgiveness, which Paul describes in verses 11–14. He says we have passed from spiritual death to spiritual life through forgiveness of our transgressions (v. 13). In verse 14 he draws a vivid picture of that forgiveness, saying Christ has "canceled out the certificate of debt consisting of decrees against us and which was hostile to us; and He has taken it out of the way, having nailed it to the cross." When someone was crucified, a list of his crimes was often nailed to the cross directly above his head. His death was payment for those crimes. The crimes that nailed Jesus to the cross were not His but ours. Because He bore our penalty, God erased the certificate of debt against us.

To complete salvation and complete forgiveness, Paul adds a third thought: complete victory (v. 15). In His death and resurrection Christ triumphed over demonic forces, thereby giving us victory over the evil one himself.

In Christ we have complete salvation, complete forgiveness, and complete victory—comprehensive resources for every issue of life. That's true sufficiency! What can philosophy add to that?

Christ Plus Legalism

Many years ago a college acquaintance said to me, "I don't think you're a very spiritual person."

I was puzzled because he didn't know me well enough to draw that kind of conclusion, so I asked him why he said that.

"Because you don't go to mid-week prayer meetings," he answered.

"What does that have to do with my spirituality?" I responded. "For all you know I might spend all day and all night in prayer."

"No," he said. "Spiritual people attend prayer meetings."

If he had said spiritual people pray, I would have agreed and confessed that I needed to pray more faithfully and fervently. But condemning someone for not keeping manmade rules or religious rituals is legalism. Jesus faced it often in his conflicts with the Pharisees. Paul warns about it in Colossians 2:16–17:

> Let no one act as your judge in regard to food or drink or in respect to a festival or a new moon or a Sabbath day—things which are a mere shadow of what is to come; but the substance belongs to Christ.

Paul was addressing legalistic people in the churches who believed, in effect, that a personal, vital, deep relationship with Christ alone is not enough to satisfy God. They had added rules and requirements governing the performance of certain duties that they thought were essential to spirituality—rules about eating and drinking, dress and appearance, religious rituals, and so on. In the Mosaic economy, God gave many such external laws to shield Israel from social interaction with corrupting pagan peoples as well as to illustrate internal spiritual truths that would be fulfilled in Christ.

Paul also said, "We are the true circumcision, who worship in the Spirit of God and glory in Christ Jesus and put no confidence in the flesh" (Phil. 3:3). What did he mean? Verses 4–9 answer:

> Although I myself might have confidence even in the flesh. If anyone else has a mind to put confidence in the flesh, I far more: circumcised the eighth day, of the nation of Israel, of the tribe of Benjamin, a Hebrew of Hebrews; as to the Law, a Pharisee; as to zeal, a persecutor of the church; as to the righteousness which is in the Law, found blameless. But whatever things were gain to me, those things I have counted as loss for the sake of Christ. More than that, I count all things to be loss in view of the surpassing value of knowing Christ Jesus my Lord, for whom I have suffered the loss of all things, and count them but rubbish in order that I may gain Christ, and may be found in Him, not having a righteousness of my own derived from the Law, but that which is through faith in Christ, the righteousness which comes from God on the basis of faith.

No fleshly circumcision makes one right with God, only the true cutting away of sin by salvation in Christ.

When Christ came, the ceremonial elements of the law were set aside, because He was the fulfillment of all they foreshadowed. Nevertheless, legalists in the early church insisted that all the ceremonies—including circumcision, Sabbath observance, and dietary laws—were to be maintained as standards of spirituality. Because they were not genuinely committed to loving Jesus Christ, they were left with a sanctimonious veneer rather than true spirituality.

Their legalism was in direct conflict with the teaching of Christ Himself. Jesus made clear that dietary laws were symbolic and had no inherent ability to make someone righteous when He said that nothing going into a man can defile him. It's what comes out of a person (evil thoughts, words, and other expressions of a sinful heart) that causes defilement (Mark 7:15). That was a shocking statement, because Jewish people had always believed there were certain foods that defiled the body. They had misunderstood the symbolism of the dietary laws and thought that following them could really make someone righteous.

In Acts 10 Peter had a vision of various kinds of unclean animals which God told him to kill and eat. When Peter objected because he had "never eaten anything unholy and unclean" (v. 14), a voice from heaven said, "What God has cleansed, no longer consider unholy" (v. 15). A new day had come. God was revealing to His people that the dietary laws were no longer in effect. Peter got the message (v. 28). Believers were free from the law's bondage, empowered by grace to fulfill the righteousness of the law without being enslaved to its ceremonial details. Paul summarizes the issue in Romans 14:17: "The kingdom of God is not eating and drinking, but righteousness and peace and joy in the Holy Spirit."

In 1 Timothy 4:1–5 Paul warns against those who

> fall away from the faith, paying attention to deceitful spirits and doctrines of demons, by means of the hypocrisy of liars seared in their own conscience as with a branding iron, men who forbid marriage and advocate

abstaining from foods, which God has created to be gratefully shared in by those who believe and know the truth. For everything created by God is good, and nothing is to be rejected, if it is received with gratitude; for it is sanctified by means of the word of God and prayer.

A gospel of human works is no gospel at all (Gal. 1:6–7; 5:2). If baptism, prayers, fasting, wearing special garments, church attendance, various kinds of abstinences, or other religious duties are necessary to earn salvation, then Christ's work is not truly sufficient. That makes a mockery of the gospel.

Legalism is as much a threat to the church today as it was in Colosse. Even in evangelical churches there are many people whose assurance of salvation is based on their religious activities rather than faith alone in the all-sufficient Savior. They assume they are Christians because they read the Bible, pray, go to church, or perform other religious functions. They judge spirituality on the basis of external performance rather than internal love for Christ, hatred for sin, and a heart devoted to obedience.

Obviously Bible reading, prayer, and the fellowship of believers can be manifestations of true conversion. But when isolated from devotion to the Lord Christ, they are reduced to meaningless religious rituals that even unbelievers can perform and by which they are deceived as to their coming destruction. Jesus said:

Many will say to Me on that day, "Lord, Lord, did we not prophesy in Your name, and in Your name cast out demons, and in Your name perform many miracles?" And then I will declare to them, "I never knew you; depart from Me, you who practice lawlessness." (Matt. 7:22–23)

Don't be intimidated by the superficial legalistic expectations of others. Let your behavior be the overflow of your love for Christ and the holy longings produced in you by the indwelling Spirit and the abiding presence of His Word (Col. 3:16).

Christ Plus Mysticism

The Colossian believers were also being intimidated by people who claimed to have a higher, broader, deeper, and fuller union with God than Christ alone could give. They were the mystics. They claimed to have interacted with angelic beings through visions and other mystical experiences. Paul said of them:

> Do not let anyone who delights in false humility and the worship of angels disqualify you for the prize. Such a person goes into great detail about what he has seen, and his unspiritual mind puffs him up with idle notions. He has lost connection with the Head, from whom the whole body, supported and held together by its ligaments and sinews, grows as God causes it to grow. (Col. 2:18–19, NIV)

Mysticism is still very much alive, still using spiritual intimidation to demean the uninitiated. People today who claim to have had heavenly visions or spellbinding experiences are often simply puffed up with idle notions, using their claims to intimidate others into elevating them. As the apostle Paul wrote the Colossian believers, that kind of mysticism is the product of a prideful and unspiritual mind. Those who embrace it have turned from their sufficiency in

Christ, who alone produces true spirituality. Don't be intimidated by them.

Apparently the Colossian mystics claimed that anyone *not* having similar esoteric visions or embracing similar doctrines was disqualified from obtaining the prize of true spirituality. In reality they themselves were the disqualified ones (1 Cor. 9:27).

Mysticism is the idea that direct knowledge of God or ultimate reality is achieved through personal, subjective intuition or experience apart from, or even contrary to, historical fact or objective divine revelation. Arthur Johnson, a professor at West Texas State University, elaborates:

> When we speak of a mystical experience we refer to an event that is completely within the person. It is totally subjective. . . . Although the mystic may experience it as having been triggered by occurrences or objects outside himself (like a sunset, a piece of music, a religious ceremony, or even a sex act), the mystical experience is a totally inner event. It contains no essential aspects that exist externally to him in the physical world. . . . A mystical experience is primarily an emotive event, rather than a cognitive one. . . . Its predominant qualities have more to do with emotional intensity, or "feeling tone," than with facts evaluated and understood rationally. Although this is true, it alone is a woefully inadequate way of describing the mystical experience. The force of the experience is often so overwhelming that the person having it finds his entire life changed by it. Mere emotions cannot effect such transformations.
>
> Furthermore, it is from this emotional quality that another characteristic results, namely, its "self-authenticating" nature. The mystic rarely questions the

goodness and value of his experience. Consequently, if he describes it as giving him information, he rarely questions the truth of his newly gained "knowledge." It is this claim that mystical experiences are "ways of knowing" truth that is vital to understanding many religious movements we see today.[3]

Prevalent especially in the charismatic movement, modern mysticism embraces a concept of faith that in effect rejects reality and rationality altogether. Waging war on reason and truth, it is thus in direct conflict with Christ and Scripture. It has taken hold rapidly because it promises what so many people are seeking: something more, something better, something richer, something easier—something fast and easy to substitute for a life of careful, disciplined obedience to the Word of Christ. And because so many lack certainty that their sufficiency is in Christ, mysticism has caught many Christians unaware. It has thus swept much of the church into a dangerous netherworld of confusion and false teaching.

Mysticism has created a theological climate that is largely intolerant of precise doctrine and sound biblical exegesis. Note, for example, how wildly popular it has become to speak scornfully of doctrine, systematic Bible teaching, careful exegesis, or the bold proclamation of the gospel. Absolute truth and rational certainty are currently out of vogue. Authoritative biblical preaching is decried as too dogmatic. It is rare nowadays to hear a preacher challenge popular opinion with clear teaching from God's Word and underscore the truth with a firm and settled "Thus saith the Lord."

Ironically, a new breed of self-appointed prophets has arisen. These religious quacks tout their own dreams and visions with a different phrase, "The Lord told *me*. . . ." That is mysticism, and it preys on people looking for some secret truth that will add to the simplicity of God's all-sufficient, once-for-all delivered Word.

A well-known charismatic pastor told me that sometimes in the morning when he's shaving, Jesus comes into his bathroom and puts His arm around him and they have a conversation. Does he really believe that? I don't know. Perhaps he wants people to believe he is more intimate with Christ than most of us. Whatever the case, his experience contrasts sharply with biblical accounts of heavenly visions. Isaiah was terrified when he saw the Lord and immediately confessed his sin (Isa. 6:5). Manoah feared for his life and said to his wife, "We shall surely die, for we have seen God" (Judg. 13:22). Job repented in dust and ashes (Job 42:5–6). The disciples were petrified (Luke 8:25). Peter said to Jesus, "Depart from me, for I am a sinful man, O Lord!" (Luke 5:8). Each of them was overwhelmed with a sense of sinfulness and feared judgment. How could someone casually talk and shave while in the presence of such an infinitely holy God?

A local newspaper recently told of a well-known television evangelist who was taking a nap in his home when suddenly, he claimed, Satan himself appeared, grabbed him around the neck with both hands, and tried to strangle him to death. When he cried out, his wife came running into the room and chased the devil away. That same man has reported other bizarre experiences over the years.

I frankly don't believe accounts like that. Aside from the fact that they often don't align with biblical truth, they distract people from the truth of Christ. People begin to pursue paranormal experiences, supernatural phenomena, and special revelations—as if our resources in Christ weren't enough. They spin their views of God and spiritual truth out of their own self-authenticated, self-generated feelings, which become more important to them than the Bible. They create experiences in their minds from which they develop a belief system that simply is not true, opening themselves to further deception and even demonic influences. That's the legacy of mysticism.

Mysticism also destroys discernment. Why should people think for themselves or compare what they are taught with Scripture, when their teachers claim to receive truth directly from heaven? Thus mysticism becomes a tool through which unscrupulous leaders can coerce money and honor from the flock with fabricated experiences that play on people's gullibility.

The pastor of a rather large church in our area wanted to relocate the church. The idea wasn't popular with some members of his congregation, but he convinced them that it was God's will by appealing to mysticism. He told them that on three separate occasions the Lord Himself had spoken to him instructing him to move the church to a certain location. The pastor claimed that on the third occasion the Lord said to him, "The time has come. Leave the problem to me. I will work on many hearts. Some will not understand. Some will not follow. Most will. Go, and do my bidding." That is a verbatim quote from the church's newsletter.

When the pastor presented the plan to his congregation, he likened it to Caleb and Joshua's challenge to the Israelites to enter the Promised Land (Num. 13:30). Then he added,

> If you cannot catch the vision of God's beautiful
> plan, I will understand, but it is essential that our church

be faced with this opportunity to follow His plan. If you won't go with us I will understand. I will not think of you as evil, or destructive. . . . I want us to move forward into God's plan, and I want every one of you to go with us. You will be glad you did, and God will bless you for it.

That's the classic intimidation of an appeal to mysticism! This man effectively renounced all responsibility for his plan and placed it on God. By doing so he took the decision away from his people and other church leaders and based it on his own unreliable feelings. He implied that anyone who disagreed with his plan was opposing God's will and ran the risk of incurring the same fate that the unbelieving Israelites suffered when they refused to enter Canaan!

Maybe God wanted that church to move—that's not the issue. The pastor's appeal to his own mystical, subjective, self-authenticating feelings was wrong. Scripture is clear about how such decisions must be made—on the basis of the prayerful, wise, unanimous agreement of Spirit-filled elders who search the heart of God in Scripture, not on the mystical whims of one man.

Remember Oral Roberts' infamous claim that God would kill him if listeners didn't send several million dollars to his organization? Over the years he has made similar fantastic pleas, ranging from the promises of a miracle for certain sums of money, to the claim that God would reveal to him the cure for cancer if everyone would only send several hundred dollars. That kind of extortion is made possible because too many Christians don't recognize the error of mysticism. They want to support what God is doing but they don't know how to discern things biblically. Consequently they're indiscriminate in their giving. Some send enormous sums of money in hopes of buying a miracle. By doing so they think they're demonstrating great faith, but in reality they're showing great distrust in the sufficiency of Christ. What they think of as faith in Christ is really doubt looking for proof. Such weak people are easy victims of mysticism's false promises.

Preachers who confront mystical teachings are often branded as judgmental, unloving, or divisive. Mysticism has thus cultivated a tolerance for false and careless teaching. But the biblical mandate is clear: we must "hold firmly to the trustworthy message as it has been taught, so that [we] can encourage others by sound doctrine and refute those who oppose it" (Titus 1:9, NIV).

There is no higher plane—no surpassing experience or deeper life. Christ is all and all. Cling to *Him*. Cultivate your love for *Him*. In Him alone you are complete!

Christ Plus Asceticism

One Sunday morning I was about to finish preaching when suddenly a man approached the pulpit yelling at the top of his voice, "I have something to say. I have something to say!" Before the ushers could escort him out, the tape recorder picked up what he shouted to the congregation: "You people are religious phonies—materialistic hypocrites. If you really loved God you'd get rid of your cars and your fancy houses and give all that you have to the poor. You'd serve God in poverty like Jesus did." That was his view of spirituality, and he wanted everyone to know it.

Fortunately, that kind of behavior is uncommon. But that view of spirituality is not uncommon at all. It's called asceticism, and it has threatened the church for centuries. In fact, it was one of the heretical additives that Paul warned the Colossian Christians to avoid:

> If you have died with Christ to the elementary principles of the world, why, as if you were living in the world, do you submit yourself to decrees, such as, "Do not handle, do not taste, do not touch!" (which all refer to things destined to perish with the using)—in accordance with the commandments and teachings of men? These are matters which have, to be sure, the appearance of wisdom in self-made religion and self-abasement and severe treatment of the body, but are of no value against fleshly indulgence. (Col. 2:20–23)

An ascetic is someone who lives a life of rigorous self-denial as a means to earn forgiveness from God. The extremes of asceticism are usually associated with monasticism, which appealed to people who believed that expiation of sin and thus true spirituality required abject poverty or giving up everything to become a nun or a monk.

Our Lord requires us to take up our cross and follow Him, and there are many testimonies to the blessedness of godly self-denial. Biblically it is not an attempt to gain forgiveness or spirituality through self-abasement. Rather it is the willing response of a heart dedicated to serving Christ at any cost. Asceticism is a different matter. It is motivated by pride rather than humility, and it is an attempt to accomplish in the energy of the flesh a right relationship with God, which can be brought about only by a divine transformation through faith in Jesus Christ.

Paul said that we have "died with Christ to the elementary principles of the world" (Col. 2:20). That means we aren't in bondage to any religious systems that require some kind of abstinence to make us acceptable to God. Such teachings are not wise or even helpful. On the contrary, they're deceptive and destructive because they feign wisdom and establish a false standard of spirituality—one that is "of no value against fleshly indulgence" (v. 23).

"Of no value against fleshly indulgence" is a difficult phrase to interpret. It may mean that false, legalistic standards of spirituality are of no value in combating the desires of the flesh. That's certainly true. Asceticism can't restrain the flesh. That's why so many legalistic Christians fall into gross immorality.

More likely, however, the phrase means that false standards of spirituality serve only to indulge the flesh. Self-styled asceticism elevates the flesh and makes a person proud about his sacrifices, visions, and spiritual achievements. It takes away from Christ and enslaves the ascetic to fleshly pride.

Christ Plus Nothing!

We must hold fast to Christ's sufficiency—never adding to it or taking from it. In Him are all the treasures of wisdom and knowledge (Col. 2:3). In Him dwells all the fullness of deity in bodily form (2:9). We have been made complete in Him (2:10). And nothing can ever separate us from Him (Rom. 8:35–39). What more do we need?

Some years ago I was invited to present the gospel to a group of actors and actresses at a Hollywood hotel. That was a different environment for me, but I was thankful for the opportunity to represent Christ to them. I talked for about forty-five minutes, then challenged the people to trust Christ for salvation.

Afterward a young man came up to me and shook my hand. He was a very handsome young actor from India, who had come to Hollywood seeking stardom. He said to me, "Your speech was fascinating and compelling. I want Jesus Christ in my life." I was thrilled and suggested we go into a little side room where we would have privacy to talk together and pray.

We made our way to the room and sat down. Then he said, "I'm a Muslim. I've been a Muslim all my life. Now I want to have Christ." I was somewhat overwhelmed because I had never led a Muslim to Christ and I didn't expect one to respond so easily to the gospel. I explained in more detail what it meant to open one's heart to Christ, then suggested we pray together.

As we knelt, he invited Jesus into his life. Then I prayed for him and we stood up. I was excited and he was smiling as he shook my hand firmly. But then he made a tragic and revealing statement: "Isn't it wonderful? Now I have two religions, Christianity and Islam."

Saddened by his obvious misunderstanding of the gospel, I carefully explained to him that Christianity doesn't work that way. Jesus isn't someone you simply add to whatever other religion you choose. You must turn from error to embrace Him as Lord alone (1 Thess. 1:9). Jesus Himself said, "No one can serve two masters; for either he will hate the one and love the other, or he will hold to one and despise the other" (Matt. 6:24). You give up every other master to gain Christ, who is the pearl of great price (13:44–46). He takes all of you, and you receive all of Him (16:24–26).

But like the rich young ruler who rejected Christ for the sake of holding on to his riches (Luke 18:18–23), that young actor was unwilling to exchange his false religion for the only One who could save his soul. He walked away without Christ.

Are you resting and trusting in the sufficiency of Christ? Is Christ everything to you? If so, thank Him for His fullness. If not, perhaps you've been trusting in failing, deceptive, inept human wisdom; meaningless religious rituals; or some kind of mystical experience formed in your own mind and unrelated to reality. Maybe you've been thinking that your own self-denial or self-imposed pain will somehow gain favor with God. If that's the case, put it all aside and in simple childlike faith embrace the risen Christ as your Lord and Savior. He will give you complete salvation, complete forgiveness, and complete victory. All you need in the spiritual dimension for time and eternity is found in Him. Repent of your sin and submit your life to Him!

9

A Balance
of Faith
and Effort

Work out your salvation with fear and trembling; for it is God who is at work in you, both to will and to work for His good pleasure.

Philippians 2:12–13

It is no longer I who live, but Christ lives in me.

Galatians 2:20

IF PHILOSOPHY, LEGALISM, MYSTICISM, AND asceticism are false standards of spirituality, and psychological sanctification is no sanctification at all, how then does true sanctification occur? More specifically, what is the believer's role and what is God's role? The very fact that the New Testament is replete with commands to believers assumes that we have the responsibility and resources to obey. But how much do we do and how much does God do?

That question was put to me recently after I preached to a group of Christians on the topic of spiritual discipline. I spoke for about an hour, pouring out my heart and admonishing them to pursue a zealous, diligent, spiritual walk. Afterward a woman came up to me and took exception to what I said. "I think you have it all wrong when it comes to sanctification and the believer's daily walk with Christ," she said. "Scripture says 'Not I, but Christ liveth in me.' There's no call for us to discipline ourselves or exert human effort. We are commanded to live by faith. That means we don't do anything. We simply yield to God and let Him do it all."

She was echoing a popular strain of teaching from the "deeper life" movement. The view she held has been popularized through such books as Charles Trumbull's much-reprinted *Victory in Christ*, and *How to Live the Victorious Life*, by an author who identified himself as An Unknown Christian, and *The Christian's Secret of a Happy Life*, by Hannah Whitall Smith. They teach that Christian living requires no effort on the part of believers; the power for holiness must come from Christ living within. That view contains a germ of truth: Christians *are* to live by faith, and the source of power for holy living *is* only the indwelling Christ. But the view tends to ignore an equally important truth: Scripture *does* call believers to diligent effort. The writer of Hebrews penned these words: "Each one of you [must] show the same diligence so as to realize the full assurance of hope until the end, that you may not be sluggish, but imitators of those who through faith and patience inherit the promises" (Heb. 6:11–12). And Peter called for active faith: "Applying all diligence, in your faith supply moral excellence, and in your moral excellence, knowledge; and in your knowledge, self-control, and in your self-control, perseverance, and in your perseverance, godliness; and in your godliness, brotherly kindness, and in your brotherly kindness, love" (2 Pet. 1:5–7).

The apostle Paul highlighted the paradox of our sanctification in his epistle to the Philippians. He wrote, "Work out your salvation with fear and trembling," yet he immediately added, "it is God who is at work in you, both to will and to work for His good pleasure" (2:12–13).

194

Quietism Versus Pietism

The woman who objected to my message holds a view of sanctification known as quietism. It asserts that the Christian is to be passive (quiet) in the process of spiritual growth and let God do everything. According to quietist teaching, the Christian must exert no energy or effort in the process whatsoever, for feeble human effort only hinders the working of God's power. Quietists believe Christians must simply surrender fully to the Holy Spirit (also called "yielding," "dying to self," "crucifying oneself," "mortifying the flesh," or "placing one's life on the altar"). The Spirit then moves in and lives a life of victory through us, and Christ literally replaces us ("it is no longer I who lives, but Christ lives in me"—Gal. 2:20). In its extreme variety, quietism is a spiritual passivism in which God becomes wholly responsible for the believer's behavior, and the believer feels he must never exert personal effort to pursue righteous living. Quietists have popularized the phrases, "Let go and let God," and "I can't; He can."

The opposite of quietism is pietism, which teaches that believers must work hard and practice extreme self-discipline to achieve personal piety. Pietism stresses aggressive Bible study, self-discipline, holy living through diligent obedience, and pursuit of Christian duty. Extreme pietism doesn't stop there but often adopts legalistic standards governing one's clothing, lifestyle, and so on. The Amish sects that forbid their people to use electricity, automobiles, or other modern conveniences are examples of radical pietism.

Most quietists and pietists would agree that salvation is by grace through faith in Christ alone. Their disagreement is in the area of sanctification. Quietists downplay or totally disregard the believer's effort, and thereby risk promoting spiritual irresponsibility and apathy. Pietists can tend to overemphasize human effort and thereby inflame people's pride or lapse into legalism.

Striking a Proper Balance

Look again at Paul's words to the Philippians: "So then, my beloved, just as you have always obeyed, not as in my presence only, but now much more in my absence, work out your salvation with fear and trembling; for it is God who is at work in you, both to will and to work for His good pleasure" (2:12–13).

In verse 12 Paul sounds like a pietist: "Work out your salvation with fear and trembling." In verse 13 he sounds like a quietist: "God is at work in you." *We* are working in verse 12; *God* is working in verse 13. There is a perfect balance there, but it is admittedly difficult to understand fully. Why would the apostle command us to work out our own salvation if God Himself is at work in us both to will and to work for His ultimate purposes? Paul didn't attempt to harmonize the tension between those two statements. He simply affirmed both sides of the paradox.

Such ambiguities should not trouble us. Who can understand the mind of God? His thoughts are as far above our limited understanding as the heaven is above the earth (Isa. 55:9; Deut. 29:29).

The biblical teaching about salvation contains a similar paradox. The gospel demands that we turn from sin and embrace the Lord Jesus Christ as Savior or be forever damned. It demands an act of the human will in which the sinner repents and places faith in the Person and work of Christ. Yet Scripture says salvation is all God's work (Eph. 2:8–9), and that He has chosen people for salvation before the foundation of the world (Eph. 1:4–5).

The same tension exists in Scripture's teaching about the perseverance of the saints. All believers are eternally secure because God holds us in His hand and no one can snatch us from it (John 10:27–29). No one can bring an accusation against us and nothing can separate us from His love (Rom. 8:33–35). Yet the Bible says those who inherit eternal life will be faithful to endure to the end (Matt. 10:22; 24:13; Col. 1:22–23). Ultimate salvation is guaranteed and secured by God, but not without the persevering faith of the Christian.

Coming to the matter of sanctification, it shouldn't be surprising to find yet another inexplicable union of the believer's personal effort and God's sovereign control. Philippians 2:2–13 is certainly not the only passage to speak of sanctification in those terms. In 1 Corinthians 15:10 Paul refers to his own spiritual state, saying, "By the grace of God I am what I am, and His grace toward me did not prove vain." That sounds like a quietistic position until Paul adds: "But I labored even more than all of them." That's pietistic. He closes the verse with, "Yet not I, but the grace of God with me." Quietism again. God was making Paul what he was, and Paul was working hard alongside Him. Yet he acknowledged it all was a work of God's grace in him. Thus Paul's view of sanctification was neither quietistic nor pietistic, but a perfect balance of both.

"I . . . yet not I" typifies Paul's perspective on personal holiness (Gal. 2:20, kjv). He knew well that sanctification is a symbiosis between God, who is at work in the believer, and the believer himself, who must strive for holiness. Paul never spoke of his own sanctification without acknowledging both sides. He wouldn't take credit for God's work in his life, but neither was he content to sit around idly, counting on God to do something in him apart from his active participation.

In Colossians 1:28 Paul states the direction and ultimate goal of his ministry: "We proclaim [Christ], admonishing every man and teaching every man with all wisdom, that we may present every man complete in Christ."

In verse 29 he talks about the energy behind his ministry: "And for this purpose also I labor, striving according to His power, which mightily works within me."

The language Paul uses there is graphic. The Greek word translated "labor" (*kopiaō*) speaks of working with wearisome effort—working to the point of exhaustion. The word translated "striving" (*agōnizomai*) is the word from which we get our English word *agonize*. It means "to strain," "toil," or "suffer." The word emphasizes Paul's tireless labor and his struggles against all manner of setbacks and opposition. This is not the language of a quietist.

Paul exerted maximum effort, striving, agonizing— but he adds the crucial phrase: "according to His power, which mightily works within me." That's the same marvelous and mysterious paradox we see continually in Paul's writings. Clearly the sanctification of which he wrote was the result of his working in concert with the divine purpose— but he always gave God the glory.

Holy living, then, demands that we commit our lives and energy to the service of Jesus Christ with every faculty we possess. Every command in Scripture would otherwise be meaningless. In fact, the first and great commandment calls for all-out effort: "You shall love the Lord your God with all your heart, and with all your soul, and with all your mind, and with all your strength" (Mark 12:30). And every chastening act of God on a believer affirms the gravity of that responsibility (Heb. 12:1–11). Believers must use all their energies in serving the Lord with diligence. At the same time, all that is accomplished within us is the work of God.

Our Part: Working Out Our Salvation

The main thrust of Philippians 2:12 is the phrase, "work out your salvation." The Greek verb translated "work" (*katergazomai*) is a present-tense imperative verb, and could be translated, "keep on continually making the effort to work out your salvation." That's the Christian's part in sanctification.

Some have mistakenly concluded that working out our salvation means we must earn it, that is, work *for* or *toward* it. But clearly salvation is "the gift of God; not as a result of works, that no one should boast" (Eph. 2:8–9). Further, Paul said, "By the works of the Law no flesh will be justified. . . . For all have sinned and fall short of the glory of God, being justified as a gift by His grace through the redemption which is in Christ Jesus. . . . For we maintain that a man is justified by faith apart from works of the Law" (Rom. 3:20, 23–24, 28).

"Work out your salvation" is not a command for unbelievers to work *for* their salvation. It is a call to believers for sustained effort and diligence in holy living based on the divine resources within them (Phil. 2:13). Scripture is replete with such injunctions. For example Romans 6:19 says, "Just as you presented your members as slaves to impurity and to lawlessness, resulting in further lawlessness, so now present your members as slaves to righteousness, resulting in sanctification." Second Corinthians 7:1 says, "Let us cleanse ourselves from all defilement of the flesh and spirit, perfecting holiness in the fear of God." Paul said to the Ephesians, "Walk in a manner worthy of the calling with which you have been called" (Eph. 4:1) and he detailed how to accomplish that (vv. 2–3). In Colossians 3:5–17 he gives a list of injunctions that imply our responsibility to cultivate spiritual discipline and holy living.

In 1 Corinthians 9:24–27 Paul says, "Do you not know that those who run in a race all run, but only one receives the prize? Run in such a way that you may win. And everyone who competes in the games exercises self-control in all things. . . . Therefore I run in such a way, as not without aim; I box in such a way, as not beating the air; but I buffet my body and make it my slave, lest possibly after I have preached to others, I myself should be disqualified." Paul didn't shadow box or run in circles. He fought to win. He pursued holiness with maximum effort. At the end of his life he proclaimed with confidence, "I have fought the good fight, I have finished the course, I have kept the faith" (2 Tim. 4:7).

The command to work out our salvation also speaks of striving toward a goal, or bringing something to fulfillment, fullness, or completion, just as you might "work out" a difficult problem or a pianist might "work out" a difficult phrase of a sonata. The expression speaks of resolving something, perfecting it, or bringing it to completion. Paul wanted the Philippians to push their salvation to perfection in Christlikeness. When he speaks of salvation, he is seeing the fullness of its fruition, urging the Philippians to press on to that goal. In other words, the sense of Paul's message is not "work *for* your salvation," but "work *on* your salvation" in the sense of moving toward faith's consummation in glory. The elect are diligently to pursue holiness until Christ returns.

Philippians 2:12 contains five key phrases that help us understand how to work out our salvation: "So then, my beloved, just as you have always obeyed, not as in my presence only, but now much more in my absence, work out your salvation with fear and trembling."

"So Then": Understand Your Example. "So then" refers back to Philippians 2:5–11, which presents Jesus Christ as the model of humility, obedience, and submission:

> Have this attitude in yourselves which was also in Christ Jesus, who, although He existed in the form of God, did not regard equality with God a thing to be grasped, but emptied Himself, taking the form of a bond-servant, and being made in the likeness of men. And being found in appearance as a man, He humbled Himself by becoming obedient to the point of death, even death on a cross.
>
> Therefore also God highly exalted Him, and bestowed on Him the name which is above every name, that at the name of Jesus every knee should bow, of those who are in heaven, and on earth, and under the earth, and that every tongue should confess that Jesus Christ is Lord, to the glory of God the Father.

Christlikeness is the substance of spiritual dedication. That's why Paul told the Galatians he was in labor until Christ was fully formed in them (Gal. 4:19), and why John said that those who claim to know Christ should follow His pattern of life (1 John 2:6).

"My Beloved": Understand You Are Loved. The Philippian church was a faithful church, but it was not without problems. Apparently there was pride and disunity in the church, otherwise Paul probably wouldn't have stressed unity so strongly (2:1–5). We know that two women, Euodia and Syntyche, led factions that were at odds with each other (4:2–3), and undoubtedly there were other such problems.

Despite the Philippians' failures, Paul still loved and patiently corrected them. He called them "beloved" (Phil. 2:12; 4:1). In 1:8 he says, "I long for you all with the affection of Christ Jesus." He treated them with the patience, mercy, and grace that are indicative of Christ Himself.

In the process of working out your salvation, there will be times when you fail. Therefore you need to understand that God loves you and is patient, merciful, and forgiving toward you. There is room within His love for your failures.

"Just as You Have Always Obeyed": Understand the Place of Obedience. Obedience is the hallmark of all who truly love Christ (John 14:15). The Philippians were no exception. The Greek word translated "obeyed" (*hupakouō*) literally means "to answer the door," or "obey as a result of listening." It carries the idea of submitting to something you've heard. Lydia, for example, listened to Paul's preaching at Philippi and the Lord opened her heart to respond to the gospel. Subsequently she was baptized and extended hospitality to Paul and his companions (Acts 16:14–15). The same was true of the Philippian jailer in verses 30–34. Each responded to God's Word.

"Not as in My Presence Only, but Now Much More in My Absence": Understand Your Resources and Responsibilities. The Philippian believers were obedient when Paul was

with them, but he wanted them to excel even more in his absence. In one sense they no longer needed him. It was time for them to internalize his teachings and continue pursuing godliness on their own. That's the responsibility of all Christians.

The loving support and accountability that other believers bring to our lives is a wonderful thing, but it is possible to lean too heavily on others for spiritual strength and encouragement. Sometimes when Christians leave that kind of supportive environment, they struggle with discipline and purity because their spiritual props and godly peer pressure are gone.

When Paul said, "work out *your* salvation" (emphasis added), he implied that the saints are sufficient in Christ to pursue godliness apart from any external support. They are self-contained repositories of all the divine resources and are both capable and responsible for their own spiritual well-being.

"With Fear and Trembling": Understand the Consequences of Sin. Although God is patient and forgiving when His children sin, sin inevitably has consequences. That's why we must pursue sanctification "with fear and trembling."

The Greek term rendered "fear" is *phobos*, from which the English word *phobia* comes. "Trembling" is from *tromos*, which is the origin of the word *trauma*. Together those words speak of a healthy fear of offending God and a proper anxiety to do what is right in His eyes. It is not a fear of eternal doom but a reverential awe that motivates a person to righteousness.

This kind of fear is fear of sinning, distrust of one's own strength in the face of temptation, horror at the thought of dishonoring God. It is a sense of foreboding that comes with understanding the deceitfulness of sin and the unreliability of one's own heart. It is terror at the thought of a moral breakdown; a loathing of the disqualification such

203

sin might cause; and the kind of circumspection Paul enjoined when he reminded the early church of the failures of the Israelites. It is a moral revulsion at anything that would grieve or cause affront to a thrice-holy God.

Isaiah 66:2 speaks of righteous fear: "To this one I will look, / To him who is humble and contrite of spirit, and who trembles at My word." Verse 5 says, "Hear the word of the Lord, you who tremble at His word." When the Lord speaks in this context of a trembler at His Word, He is, in effect, using that expression as a title for the true believer. Every believer should live in such awe of God's majesty and holiness that he shuns sin lest it grieve his Lord, violate his testimony to an unbelieving world, or negate his usefulness for ministry in the body of Christ and bring divine chastening.

Working out our salvation is not easy. It takes hard, consistent effort and discipline. It involves a lifelong pursuit of holiness that requires following the example of Christ, understanding the love of God, cultivating obedience to the Word of God, appropriating your spiritual resources, and appreciating the serious consequences of sin.

Paul said it called for beating our bodies into submission (1 Cor. 9:27) and cleansing ourselves from all filthiness of the flesh, perfecting holiness in the fear of God (2 Cor. 7:1). A high calling like that will mean all will fail at times. But a healthy fear of God will restrain such failure, because it motivates us to pursue godliness above all else.

God's Part: Working in Us

In Philippians 2:13 Paul explains God's part in sanctification: "It is God who is at work in you, both to will and to work for His good pleasure." What a remarkable truth! God Himself indwells us and empowers us to do His will. We are not adequate in ourselves, but our adequacy is from God (2 Cor. 3:5). Within that brief verse are five key truths about God that will help us understand our divine resources for Christian living.

His Person: God. Paul said, "It is *God* who is at work in you" (emphasis added). The literal Greek places the emphasis on God: "God is the one at work in you." God is so intimately involved in your life and so concerned about your spiritual well-being that He personally indwells you to effect what He commands.

The energy behind your spiritual progress is not your human abilities or resources, although God might bless you with an abundance of both. Nor is it the encouragement and support of other Christians, although the ministry of fellow believers is certainly a great blessing. It isn't human pastors and teachers who instruct you in God's Word and care for you as a shepherd cares for his sheep. It isn't even the holy angels who are sent forth from heaven as ministering spirits (Heb. 1:14).

The real cause of all spiritual progress is this alone: God Himself is working within you to effect your sanctification. That's why sanctification can never be totally deterred. The same God who justifies you sanctifies you and will ultimately glorify you (Rom. 8:30). Salvation will always produce the fruit of righteousness (James 2:17–26; Eph. 2:10). It's inevitable; the unchanging, glorious, sovereign, majestic, righteous, holy, gracious, and merciful God, the God who rules all things and always does what He desires— that God is at work in you, and He is never thwarted.

That's an unimaginable concept to a pagan world, whose gods are largely uncaring, uninvolved, and vengeful.

But our God works in us because He loves us with an everlasting love and extends eternal kindness to us. He keeps us with an everlasting covenant based on everlasting promises. "The gifts and the calling of God are irrevocable" (Rom. 11:29). He sees us through to the end and supplies all our needs in Christ Jesus.

His Power: At Work. Paul used the present participle form of the Greek verb *energeō* to describe God's activity within us: "It is God who is *at work* in you" (emphasis added). That's where the English word *energy* comes from. It speaks of an effectual and productive energy, the infinite power of God Himself in action. God is the One who energizes our spiritual progress. His power drives our sanctification. It compels righteousness and controverts sin. That's why we're eternally secure in Christ. His power continues to drive us to glorification. We persevere because we are energized by Him. Since there is no limit to His power, we know He will ultimately complete what He has begun in us (Phil. 1:6).

His Presence: In You. In Ephesians 3:20 Paul says that God is "able to do exceeding abundantly beyond all that we ask or think, according to the power that works within us." He could have said "according to the power that works in heaven, or in Christ, or in the Holy Spirit." But instead he stressed God's power at work in *us*. God can and does accomplish purposes through His power at work in us that are beyond our ability to plan, reason, or even dream. That inner power flows from God Himself and is the basis of our sufficiency.

By the way, God's presence within believers is a uniquely Christian doctrine. In the Old Testament, believers worshiped God in the tabernacle or at the Temple. Because Christ indwells believers in this age; we are His temple.

Second Corinthians 6:16–17 says, "We are the temple of the living God; just as God said, 'I will dwell in them and walk with them; / And I will be their God, and they shall be My people." There is never a moment of your existence, from the time you give your life to Christ until you meet Him face to face, that God is not with you—He's always present, always supporting, always sustaining, always upholding, always supplying, always strengthening, always shielding, and always producing sanctifying effects in your life.

And that sanctifying process can't be halted. The convoluted routes some people take on their spiritual journeys may be hard to understand, but the real issue is God's faithfulness, not our carelessness. Sin will slow the process but God will accomplish His purposes even if He has to chasten the believer to do it (Heb. 12:5–11).

His Purpose: To Will and to Work. God's purpose is to energize our will and our work—our desires and our deeds. His power gives us both the desire and the ability to do what is right.

All behavior rises out of desires and intentions. In fact, the Greek word translated "to will" (*thelō*) in Philippians 2:13 speaks of intent or inclination. God works in us to instill godly desires so our behavior will be pleasing to Him.

How does He do that? By using two things to conform our desires to His. The first is holy discontent. God makes us dissatisfied with our fleshly nature. Paul experienced that to the point of misery when he cried out, "Wretched man that I am! Who will set me free from the body of this death?" (Rom. 7:24). He wasn't discontent with his circumstances, but with his sin.

The second thing God uses to conform our desires to His is holy aspiration. That's the flip side of discontent.

207

It's a longing for something better, purer, and more holy. We read about men of God like Paul or John and our hearts are filled with an aspiration to be like them. Or we might read a biography of some great servant of the Lord and suddenly realize how shallow our commitment is by comparison. That generates a holy aspiration to be more available for God's use.

In addition to energizing our desires and intents, God also energizes us to work for His good pleasure. Paul used the same Greek word to describe our work as he used to describe God's (*energeō*). God energizes us for the things that please Him. Holy discontent leads to holy aspiration, which leads to a holy resolve to do what is right. That leads ultimately to holy behavior.

His Pleasure: For His Good Pleasure. The Greek noun translated "pleasure" (*eudokia*) in Philippians 2:13 speaks of satisfaction or good pleasure. God works in us to cause us to do what satisfies and pleases Him. Such is the goal of the sanctification process. Working out our salvation with fear and trembling pleases Him.

Believers are very dear to God; so when we obey His will, He is pleased. Isn't that the essence of a relationship? We want to please the ones we love. God wants our best because that's what pleases Him most—and He is worthy of even more—so we should give Him our best as a demonstration of our love.

Think of it! We can bring pleasure to the One who does everything for us—who pardons all our iniquities; who heals all our spiritual afflictions; who redeems our lives from the pit; who crowns us with lovingkindness and compassion; who satisfies our years with good things, so that our youth is renewed like the eagle (Ps. 103:3–5). What an immense privilege!

So rather than taking a purely quietistic or pietistic approach to sanctification, we see there's to be a wonderful blend of our best efforts and God's resources. We do not serve an overbearing and forceful God who makes impossible demands, then crushes us for our non-compliance. We serve a God who empowers us to live to His glory.

The uniqueness and mystery of Christianity is "Christ in you, the hope of glory" (Col. 1:27). He is our sanctification and our sufficiency. God calls us to holiness and then makes us holy. He calls us to serve and then mobilizes us to serve by His own power and presence. It is His work, and it is our work—a divine partnership. But the glory belongs to Him alone.

In that there is absolute sufficiency! No matter what the issue of life, the source to turn to is God! Who but a fool would settle for less?

10

Spiritual Warfare: Who's After Whom?

Put on the full armor of God, that you may be able to stand firm against the schemes of the devil. For our struggle is not against flesh and blood, but against the rulers, against the powers, against the world forces of this darkness, against the spiritual forces of wickedness in the heavenly places.

Ephesians 6:11–12

THIS ARTICLE APPEARED RECENTLY IN THE
Los Angeles Times:

Under the militant banner of "spiritual warfare," growing numbers of evangelical and charismatic Christian leaders are preparing broad assaults on what they call the cosmic powers of darkness.

Fascinated with the notion that Satan commands a hierarchy of territorial demons, some mission agencies and big-church pastors are devising strategies for "breaking the strongholds" of those evil spirits alleged to be controlling cities and countries.

Some proponents in the fledgling movement already maintain that focused prayer meetings have ended the curse of the Bermuda Triangle, led to the 1987 downfall in Oregon of free-love guru Baghwan Shree Rajneesh and, for the 1984 Summer Olympics in Los

Angeles, produced a two-week drop in the crime rate, a friendly atmosphere and unclogged freeways.

This is not the cinematic story line for a religious sequel to "Ghostbusters II," yet the developing scenario does have a fictional influence: interest in spiritual warfare has been heightened by two best-selling novels in Christian bookstores. "This Present Darkness," by Frank Peretti, describes the religious fight against "territorial spirits mobilized to dominate a small town." A second Peretti novel has a similar premise.

Fuller Seminary Prof. C. Peter Wagner, who has written extensively on the subject, led a "summit" meeting on cosmic-level spiritual warfare Monday in Pasadena with two dozen men and women, including a Texas couple heading a group called the "Generals of Intercession" and an Oregon man who conducts "spiritual warfare boot camps."

In his opening remarks, Wagner said: "The [Holy] Spirit is saying something to churches through these [Peretti] books even though they are fiction. People are reading these books that would never read our books. . . .

[A] cause for caution, said Wagner, is the danger involved: "If you do not know what you are doing, and few . . . have the necessary expertise, Satan will eat you for breakfast."[1]

I am amazed at the number of Christians being drawn into the burgeoning "spiritual warfare" movement. I am convinced it represents an unhealthy obsession with Satan and demonic powers. Judging from the turnouts, thousands of Christians really believe that if they don't attend a spiritual-warfare boot camp and learn some strategy for fighting demons, Satan will have them for breakfast.

Is that true? Is there some secret strategy to be learned from "experts" in the art of spiritual warfare? Do Christians need to study mystic techniques for confronting and commanding evil forces, "binding" the devil, "breaking the strongholds" of territorial demons, and other complex stratagems of metaphysical combat? Is it simplistic to think that the basic armor described in Ephesians 6 is sufficient to keep us from being breakfast for Satan?

Absolutely not. One of the glorious truths of our sufficiency in Christ is that we are already more than conquerors in the great cosmic spiritual warfare (Rom. 8:37). Satan is an already defeated foe (Col. 2:15; 1 Pet. 3:22).

Certainly we are involved in an ongoing "struggle . . . against the rulers, against the powers, against the world forces of this darkness, against the spiritual forces of wickedness in the heavenly places" (Eph. 6:12). But Christ is already the Victor in this spiritual war. When the apostle Paul wrote to the Ephesian Christians, he was not suggesting that they view their conflict with the powers of darkness as a battle whose outcome still hung in the balance. He was telling them they needed to "be strong in the Lord, and in the strength of *His* might" (v. 10, emphasis added); to "stand firm" (vv. 11, 13); to use the spiritual armor—truth, righteousness, the gospel of peace, faith, salvation, and God's Word—to resist the schemes of the devil. They were to fight from a position of victory, not out of fear that Satan might make them toast.

Nor was the apostle suggesting that the church should initiate confrontations with evil principalities and powers. There's no need for Christians to seek to engage Satan in combat. Nowhere in Scripture are we ever encouraged to do so. On the contrary, we are to "be of sober spirit, [and] be on the alert," for *he* prowls around like a roaring, devouring lion (1 Pet. 5:8, emphasis added). After all, who is after whom?

Since Satan is pursuing us, how do we keep from becoming instant breakfast? Certainly not by chasing after him, hunting him down, attempting to bind him, commanding him, or rebuking him with some incantation. We simply "resist the devil and he will flee" (James 4:7). Why? Because the One who indwells every believer is greater than the devil (1 John 4:4)—and all the powers of hell know it (Matt. 8:28–32).

That a movement so obsessed with Satan and his minions could suddenly gain such popularity among Bible-believing Christians is proof of the influence mysticism has had in the church. Many of the tactics these self-styled experts in spiritual warfare are advocating have no scriptural warrant whatsoever. They are the fruit of mysticism run amok. Those who advocate them speak as if they had great authority, but the truth is you won't find biblical support for most of the techniques they recommend. Where does Scripture indicate, for example, that Christians should band together to wage prayer wars against crime and traffic jams or exorcise phenomena like the Bermuda Triangle?

Worst of all, such teaching actually encourages Christians to dabble in demonic affairs or to live in fear and superstition. That is exactly contrary to God's design. We are to equip ourselves for spiritual warfare by becoming experts in righteousness, not by focusing our thoughts and energies on the enemy and fearing his power (Phil. 4:8; Rom. 16:19).

To put it another way, our sufficiency in Christ fits us for the battle. The spiritual resources we gain in Him are sufficient to sustain us in the face of the enemy—apart from any maneuvers that might be learned in some spiritual warfare seminar. "We are not ignorant of his schemes" (2 Cor. 2:11); we have a greater power indwelling us (1 John 4:4); and we have God's own promise of absolute security in Christ (Rom. 8:38–39).

Let's take an extended look at what Scripture teaches about spiritual warfare:

The Participants

When we use the term *spiritual warfare,* what are we talking about? Who is battling whom? And why? Revelation 12 tells the whole story in a single narrative. This is the apostle John's vision of the cosmic warfare of the ages:

> And a great sign appeared in heaven: a woman clothed with the sun, and the moon under her feet, and on her head a crown of twelve stars; and she was with child; and she cried out, being in labor and in pain to give birth. And another sign appeared in heaven: and behold, a great red dragon having seven heads and ten horns, and on his heads were seven diadems. And his tail swept away a third of the stars of heaven, and threw them to the earth. And the dragon stood before the woman who was about to give birth, so that when she gave birth he might devour her child. And she gave birth to a son, a male child, who is to rule all the nations with a rod of iron; and her child was caught up to God and to His throne. And the woman fled into the wilderness where she had a place prepared by God, so that there she might be nourished for one thousand two hundred and sixty days.

217

And there was war in heaven, Michael and his angels waging war with the dragon. And the dragon and his angels waged war, and they were not strong enough, and there was no longer a place found for them in heaven. And the great dragon was thrown down, the serpent of old who is called the devil and Satan, who deceives the whole world; he was thrown down to the earth, and his angels were thrown down with him. And I heard a loud voice in heaven, saying, "Now the salvation, and the power, and the kingdom of our God and the authority of His Christ have come, for the accuser of our brethren has been thrown down, who accuses them before our God day and night. And they overcame him because of the blood of the Lamb and because of the word of their testimony, and they did not love their life even to death. For this reason, rejoice, O heavens and you who dwell in them. Woe to the earth and the sea, because the devil has come down to you, having great wrath, knowing that he has only a short time."

And when the dragon saw that he was thrown down to the earth, he persecuted the woman who gave birth to the male child. And the two wings of the great eagle were given to the woman, in order that she might fly into the wilderness to her place, where she was nourished for a time and times and half a time, from the presence of the serpent. And the serpent poured water like a river out of his mouth after the woman, so that he might cause her to be swept away with the flood. And the earth helped the woman, and the earth opened its mouth and drank up the river which the dragon poured out of his mouth. And the dragon was enraged with the woman, and went off to make war with the rest of her offspring, who keep the commandments of God and hold to the testimony of Jesus.

Thus the lines are drawn. But who are these persons? "The dragon and his angels," "Michael and his angels," a woman and her son? Whom do they represent? The symbolism is not difficult to interpret. This account perfectly harmonizes with all that Scripture teaches about the history of the universe.

The great red dragon is identified in verse 9: he is Satan. His seven heads and ten horns correspond with other elements of the book of Revelation, and they mark him as the principal leader of all anti-Christian activity.

Verse 4 speaks of his tail sweeping away a third of the stars of heaven. That also is interpreted in verse 9. The stars refer to fallen angels—evidently angels who joined Lucifer's rebellion against God and were thrown from heaven. We know them as demons.

Note that on Satan's side are one-third of the total number of angels. Elsewhere in Scripture (Jude 6), we learn that some of the fallen angels are bound in everlasting chains (KJV). So the satanic force is diminished from its original one-third.

Two-thirds of the angels were not cast from heaven. These holy angels are aligned with Michael the archangel, chief of God's host. We are not told an actual number, but it must be very, very large. Revelation 5:11 says there are "myriads of myriads" of angels around God's throne. The Greek text uses a term for the largest number the language could express—ten thousand. "Myriads of myriads" would thus be multiplied ten thousands; more than millions, perhaps more than billions—actually a number so high it is hard to express.

If that's how many holy angels there are, there are fewer than half as many fallen angels—but still an enormous number.

Michael, the champion and leader of the holy angels, is mentioned three times in Scripture: here, in Jude 9, and in the book of Daniel. He is an archangel, a kind of super-angel. He is the dragon's counterpart, the most powerful of God's angels and commander of the heavenly host.

The woman in verse 4 is Israel. Her child is the Messiah: He "is to rule all the nations with a rod of iron; and her child was caught up to God and to His throne" (v. 5). This woman is not Mary, our Lord's earthly mother, because in John's vision "the woman fled into the wilderness where she had a place prepared by God, so that there she might be nourished for one thousand two hundred and sixty days" (v. 6). That is descriptive of the nation of Israel, which will be severely persecuted in the Great Tribulation.

Satan's Targets

Who are the targets of the dragon's wrath? The primary one was the woman's child: "The dragon stood before the woman who was about to give birth, so that when she gave birth he might devour her child" (v. 4). This is Jesus Christ. The Old Testament records a number of ways Satan unsuccessfully endeavored to destroy the messianic line so Christ could not even be born. At the Savior's birth, Herod issued a decree to find the Child and slay Him. That was a satanic plot. When it didn't work, the devil tried to conquer Jesus in the wilderness (Matt. 4:1–11; Luke 4:1–13). At the cross, the dragon may have thought he finally had devoured the woman's Child, but Christ gloriously rose from the dead. After forty days He ascended into heaven. As Revelation 12:5 says, "Her child was caught up to God and to His throne."

So the dragon turned his attention to a second target—Israel. Again, in the Old Testament there are a number of accounts that describe Satan's unsuccessful efforts to destroy Israel. Israel's history since A.D. 70 is a chronicle of persecution and holocaust. The powers of darkness have furiously tried to wipe her out, knowing that the nation of Israel is crucial in God's eternal plan because of the covenant He made with Abraham. The mass murder of Jews under Hitler's regime was only the latest in many centuries of demonically motivated persecution borne by the Jewish people.

The dragon has a third target: the holy angels. Verse 7 says, "There was war in heaven, Michael and his angels waging war with the dragon. And the dragon and his angels waged war." Satan's aim again is to hinder the work of Christ. Since the angels are ministering spirits who serve the Lord (Heb. 1:14), the demonic forces attack them (note Daniel 10:13). Of course, just as they failed to destroy Christ, demons could never totally thwart His work; but they hate Him and all He stands for with a hellish passion, so they oppose His agents.

This is serious war. We learn from Scripture that the angels don't treat Satan flippantly. Jude tells us that when Moses died, Satan and Michael contended over his body. What did Satan want with Moses' body? Who knows? Perhaps he planned to fabricate some lie that would cause people to believe Moses was still living and put a satanic message in his mouth. But God would not allow anything like that to happen. He sent Michael to deal with Satan.

Jude 9 tells us, "Michael the archangel, when he disputed with the devil and argued about the body of Moses, did not dare pronounce against him a railing judgment, but said, 'The Lord rebuke you.'" Even this most powerful of the holy angels did not presume to rail against Satan. Why? Because Michael knew his only sufficiency was God. He was not Satan's master. So he said, "The *Lord* rebuke you."

Note also that the warfare described in Revelation 12 far transcends the realm of individual humans. There are no time or space limitations in the apostle John's vision. Its arena is another dimension. This warfare takes place on a cosmic level that—while it certainly does not exclude the world of humanity—is far beyond our ability to understand or master.

Believers' Role in the Warfare

Revelation 12 *does* mention human participants in the great cosmic battle. They appear in verse 10, when a loud voice in heaven shouts, "Now the salvation, and the power, and the kingdom of our God and the authority of His Christ have come, for the accuser of our brethren has been thrown down, who accuses them before our God day and night." The "brethren" there are Christians, for the next verse goes on to say, "And they overcame him because of the blood of the Lamb and because of the word of their testimony, and they did not love their life even to death."

We see examples of demonic attack against Christians throughout the New Testament. Now that may surprise you if you have been influenced by those who advocate speaking to demons, "binding" them, commanding them, and so on; but often those who were most effective in the Lord's service were subject to the most persistent satanic attacks. Paul, for example, wrote in 2 Corinthians 12,

For this reason, to keep me from exalting myself, there was given me a thorn in the flesh, a messenger of Satan to buffet me—to keep me from exalting myself! Concerning this I entreated the Lord three times that it might depart from me. And He has said to me, "My grace is sufficient for you, for power is perfected in weakness." Most gladly, therefore, I will rather boast about my weaknesses, that the power of Christ may dwell in me (vv. 7–9).

This is a fascinating passage for several reasons. First, note that the Greek word for "thorn" does not refer to a little spine that pricks your finger; it is a stake. Paul says it was driven right through his flesh to impale him. That is painful, excruciating imagery!

Observe also that the apostle did not rebuke the messenger of Satan, bind him, charge him to do anything in Jesus' name—he didn't even speak to him! He didn't use any of the methods championed by those in the spiritual warfare movement today. He prayed to the Lord!

Moreover, he did not get the answer he wanted. Though he was an apostle, he evidently did not feel he had spiritual authority to "claim" victory or healing or to command Satan to do what he wanted. He simply trusted the Lord and endured the satanic thorn in his flesh, knowing that God's purposes are always righteous. We'll examine this monumental text more closely in the following chapter.

First Thessalonians 2:17–18 relates another incident where Paul was frustrated by Satan. There Paul says, "We, brethren, having been bereft of you for a short while—in person, not in spirit—were all the more eager with great desire to see your face. For we wanted to come to you—I, Paul, more than once—and yet Satan thwarted us." Paul, the apostle, could not overrule whatever obstacle it was that Satan had used to impede him from visiting the Thessalonians. On this occasion at least, Paul could not bind Satan, cast him down, break his strongholds, build a hedge to stop him, or otherwise veto his efforts to thwart him.

If the apostle Paul didn't have that power, it is sheer folly for people today to claim that they do. Paul couldn't rebuke Satan. Michael the archangel wouldn't rebuke Satan. Zechariah tells us that even the preincarnate Christ Himself, in an Old Testament battle with the devil, did not rebuke Satan directly.

We read this account in Zechariah 3:1–2:

> Then he showed me Joshua the high priest standing before the angel of the Lord [this is the Old Testament expression used of Christophanies—extraordinary appearances of our Lord on earth in human form prior to His incarnation], and Satan standing at his right hand to accuse him. And the Lord [in His preincarnate form] said to Satan, "The Lord rebuke you, Satan! Indeed, the Lord who has chosen Jerusalem rebuke you! Is this not a brand plucked from the fire?"

Here's an Old Testament picture of spiritual warfare: Joshua, the godly high priest; Christ, in a preincarnate appearance; and Satan, ready to accuse the high priest. When the Lord speaks to Satan, his words are identical to what Jude tells us Michael the archangel said: "The Lord rebuke you, Satan!" He adds, "Indeed, the Lord who has chosen Jerusalem rebuke you."

How does that image fit the teaching of people today who say believers should rebuke Satan? The truth is, these people have no clue what they're doing. All their railing against the devil has no effect. We can't rebuke Satan. We can cry out to God and ask *Him* to rebuke the devil. But we can't say, "Satan, *I* rebuke you!" What is he going to say? "Oh, I'm rebuked"? Do we think we can simply say, "I bind you Satan!" and expect him to respond, "Oops, that's the end of that"? If I had that kind of authority over the adversary, I'd silence him permanently and put an end to his diabolical interference forever!

Can you see the folly of such thinking? It is absurd to think we can command Satan. There is only One who can. If even the apostle Paul could be thwarted by Satan and his messenger with a thorn, who are we to think we can talk to the devil and expect him to obey? If Paul had to trust God to take care of Satan, what makes us think we can step in and take over the fight?

Satan's Strategy

We need to understand Satan's strategy. One of his prime objectives is to blind unbelievers. Second Corinthians 4:3–4 says, "If our gospel is veiled, it is veiled to those who are perishing, in whose case the god of this world has blinded the minds of the unbelieving, that they might not see the light of the gospel of the glory of Christ, who is the image of God." "The god of this world" refers to Satan. He wants to blind unbelievers through ignorance, unbelief, false religion, love of sin, fleshly gratification—whatever means he can use.

Second, his strategy is to tempt believers. Just as he tempted Christ three times, he uses all his wiles and subtlety to tempt the elect. But please understand, every time we are tempted it is not necessarily the work of the devil. James 1:14–15 says, "Each one is tempted when he is carried away and enticed by his own lust. Then when lust has conceived, it gives birth to sin." James 4:1–2 says, "What is the source of quarrels and conflicts among you?" The devil? No. "Is not the source your pleasures that wage war in your members? You lust and do not have; so you commit murder. And you are envious and cannot obtain; so you fight and quarrel." We are perfectly capable of falling to temptation with no help whatsoever from the devil.

Satan, however, has built into the very fabric of this world system all the vehicles necessary to make the most of temptation. As "the god of this world" (2 Cor. 4:4), he orchestrates the world and keeps its sinister machinery effective. Does he ever personally tempt people? Yes. Ananias and Sapphira are examples from the early church. Paul said to Ananias, "Why has Satan filled your heart to lie to the Holy Spirit?" (Acts 5:3).

Satan uses everything in the world: "the lust of the flesh and the lust of the eyes and the boastful pride of life" (1 John 2:16) as the tools of his temptation. Since we are not apostles receiving divine revelation like Peter did, how can we know if temptation is from Satan himself, if a demon is causing it, or if it is just growing out of our own fleshly lusts? We can't. But does it really matter? No. Our response is the same in any case: resist.

Satan's strategy also includes accusing believers. Revelation 12:10 refers to him as "the accuser of the brethren" and says he "accuses them before our God day and night." In Zechariah's vision of Joshua the high priest, Satan was "before the angel of the Lord, and Satan standing at his right hand *to accuse him*" (Zech. 3:1, emphasis added). Satan does his best to tempt believers, then tries to accuse them before God.

God's Sovereign Purpose

Why would God allow the devil, an already defeated enemy, to continue to trouble believers? Scripture doesn't attempt to answer that question; it only assures us that God's purposes are always righteous, holy, good—and ultimately for our benefit. The devil is often useful in those purposes.

Did you realize that sometimes God sends Satan to do the Lord's work? It's true. Paul wrote of the divine purpose in the messenger of Satan that troubled him with the thorn: "to keep me from exalting myself!" (2 Cor. 12:7). He understood that God was using a satanic messenger to accomplish his humbling, which was for the glory of God.

Certainly this is another reason it is so ridiculous to try to control the devil: If we could throw him out anytime we wanted, we might foil the divine plan.

Job, perhaps the earliest of all the books in the Bible, is the classic Old Testament study in how God uses Satan's diabolical efforts to accomplish His own divine purposes. There was no one else like Job on earth—God Himself testified to that. He was "a blameless and upright man, fearing God and turning away from evil" (1:8). What God permitted Satan to do to Job is difficult for us to comprehend. He gave Satan permission to destroy all Job's possessions, his family, his health—everything, as long as he spared his life (2:6).

You know the story. Job lost everything. His children were all killed; he suffered a painful and humiliating disease; he struggled with doubt, depression, discouragement, and extreme frustration. He had to endure a procession of foolish counselors and their bad advice. Worst of all, through the whole ordeal he did not know why he was suffering. He knew nothing of the drama that was being played out in heaven.

Even if he had, he might have wondered if God was really on his side. Why would God permit Satan to do such things to Job? Scripture never tells us all the reasons, but we can discern a few. First, God, exalting His own glory before the angels, wanted to display to Satan the great security of salvation. There was nothing the powers of hell could do to overturn the character, the trust, or the faith of this man, whom God had redeemed and made righteous. Second, God wanted to strengthen Job. Read the final chapter of Job's life and you'll see that he came through his suffering even stronger, purer, more humble, and more righteous than before.

Job's story demolishes the notion that we can avoid Satan's attacks if we're sufficiently strong, or skilled enough, or trained in how to wage war against Satan. No one was more spiritually fit than Job. Yet God allowed Satan to ravage him anyway—and there was nothing Job could do about it. Job finally prevailed in the face of Satan's merciless assault, not because he found some secret way to beat the devil, not because he rebuked him or ordered him to desist, but because God was in control all along. He knew how much Job could bear. And He would not permit Satan to cross that boundary (1 Cor. 10:13). When Satan reached that limit God stopped him and his attacks ended.

Peter also was personally attacked by Satan—with God's permission. The night Jesus was taken to be crucified, the Lord had warned Peter: "Simon, Simon, behold, Satan has demanded permission to sift you like wheat" (Luke 22:31). Notice again that Satan had to get permission to attack one of God's people. Satan can't do anything to a child of God unless he gets God's consent.

Evidently Jesus did permit Satan to sift Peter, because that's exactly what happened. The devil tested him in the most extreme fashion, proving whether he was wheat or chaff. And although Peter *looked* like chaff for a while, he proved to be wheat. His faith never failed. Jesus, of course, knew it wouldn't. He told Peter, "I have prayed for you, that your faith may not fail" (v. 32).

Why did the Lord let Satan sift Peter? Partly because He wanted to show again the unbreakable strength of saving faith, bringing glory to Himself. Peter also needed to be able to strengthen other people who would face similar trials. "When once you have turned again," He told Peter in verse 32, "strengthen your brothers." And Peter came out of his ordeal stronger and wiser than ever, equipped to lead the church. He learned some indispensable lessons through his trial.

Clearly, believers are not immune from satanic opposition; nor is it God's design that we always be delivered from every evil circumstance. In Revelation 2:10 Christ warned the church at Smyrna, a righteous church suffering horrible persecution, "Do not fear what you are about to suffer. Behold, the devil is about to cast some of you into prison, that you may be tested, and you will have tribulation ten days. Be faithful until death, and I will give you the crown of life."

Why didn't the Lord simply rebuke the devil and save the believers in Smyrna from persecution? Because contrary to what many teach today, the Lord does not promise health, wealth, and prosperity. Though He assures us of ultimate victory, He does not guarantee that Satan will never attack.

We do not always know *why* He allows Satan to test or persecute us, but we can rest in the assurance that "God causes all things to work together for good to those who love God, to those who are called according to His purpose" (Rom. 8:28). You can mark this: Satan and his demons never, never act against God's people without the permission of God. And when God gives them permission, He always uses their work to accomplish some divine purpose. Often, to exalt the power of God and prove the devotion of His followers, God permits Satan to work the hardest on the noblest servants of God.

"Delivered Over to Satan"

God's purposes are not always affirmative. Sometimes He uses Satan as an instrument of judgment to punish people who are disobedient and sinful. That, too, is in harmony with God's holy purposes. Scripture gives several clear examples of this. One of the earliest is King Saul.

When Samuel anointed David as king of Israel to replace the disobedient and self-willed Saul, Scripture tells us, "The Spirit of the Lord departed from Saul, and an evil spirit from the Lord terrorized him" (1 Sam. 16:14). Saul's servants told him, "Behold now, an evil spirit from God is terrorizing you" (v. 15). They knew that if Saul was being troubled by a demon, it was occurring because God was allowing it.

Saul had opened himself to demonic influence through his own willful, hardhearted persistence in sin. He had invaded the priestly office. He had repeatedly acted in a proud and rebellious manner and thus made a mockery of all that Israel stood for. So God replaced him with a king of His own choice and allowed evil spirits to terrorize Saul. From that point on, Saul fell deeper into sin. He made bad decisions. He despised Samuel's authority. He became a proud, angry, jealous man. His style was dictatorial. He tried repeatedly to kill David. He dabbled in occult spiritism. He committed mass murder. He went insane. In the end he committed suicide.

He had given access to demonic invasion—and God permitted it to happen. What was God's purpose? Chastening. Punishment.

Judas also was tormented by the devil as a judgment for his sin. He was literally indwelt by Satan on the night he betrayed the Savior (Luke 22:3; John 13:27). He committed the most heinous crime in the history of mankind, then went out and hanged himself.

God even uses Satan to judge people in the church. Paul wrote to rebuke the Corinthians because a man in the church was living with his father's wife. Such a shocking, incestuous relationship had to be dealt with. What did Paul do? He told the Corinthians, "I have decided to deliver such a one to Satan for the destruction of his flesh, that his spirit may be saved in the day of the Lord Jesus" (1 Cor. 5:5). This man may have been a believer whose spirit would be saved but whose flesh was going to be destroyed. Or he may have been an unbeliever. Even Paul seemed unsure; he referred to him as a "so-called brother" (v. 11). Either way, the destruction of his flesh was to be carried out by Satan, but it was God's judgment on that man.

First Timothy 1:18–20 uses similar terminology. Paul wrote Timothy: "This command I entrust to you, Timothy, my son, in accordance with the prophecies previously made concerning you, that by them you may fight the good fight, keeping faith and a good conscience, which some have rejected and suffered shipwreck in regard to their faith. Among these are Hymenaeus and Alexander, whom I have delivered over to Satan, so that they may be taught not to blaspheme." Hymenaeus and Alexander may have been two of the pastors in the church at Ephesus. They had somehow failed to keep the true faith and a clear conscience. They had entered into doctrinal error and ungodliness. So Paul delivered them over to Satan so that they might learn not to blaspheme.

We don't know what happened subsequently. We have no idea how severe their judgment was. It may have taken them all the way to death. Or it simply may have been serious illness, torture, demonic torment, or some other evil. Whatever it was, it was Satan who meted it out, and he was fulfilling the perfect plan of God.

How Can We Fight the Devil?

It is clear that believers are in an intense spiritual struggle with the forces of evil. How *can* we fight back? If we have neither the authority nor the knowledge to command Satan, consign him to the pit, or otherwise rebuke him into submission, what *are* we to do?

Second Corinthians 10:3–5 is a key passage: "Though we walk in the flesh, we do not war according to the flesh, for the weapons of our warfare are not of the flesh, but divinely powerful for the destruction of fortresses. We are destroying speculations and every lofty thing raised up against the knowledge of God, and we are taking every thought captive to the obedience of Christ."

We can't fight on a human level. There aren't any fleshly techniques or words that can win a spiritual war. We must depend on spiritual weaponry and a spiritual battle plan. Our sufficiency in Christ includes weapons that are divinely powerful, that can destroy the fortresses of the spirit world and all its lofty thoughts that are raised up against the knowledge of God. What are those weapons?

They are not mystical phrases or verbal formulas. They are not the power to scold or command demons. There's nothing secret or mysterious about these weapons. They are not tricky or complicated. What are they?

Ephesians 6:13–18 is perhaps the most familiar text on the Christian's spiritual weaponry:

> Take up the full armor of God, that you may be able to resist in the evil day, and having done everything, to stand firm. Stand firm therefore, having girded your loins with *truth,* and having put on *the breastplate of righteousness,* and having shod your feet with the preparation of *the gospel of peace;* in addition to all, taking up *the shield of faith* with which you will be able to extinguish all the flaming missiles of the evil one. And take *the helmet of salvation,* and *the sword of the Spirit, which is the word of God.* With all *prayer* and petition pray at all times in the Spirit. (emphasis added)

I will not go into a detailed analysis of that passage, which I have covered fully elsewhere.[2] But observe carefully the nature of this arsenal. The pieces of armor are all spiritual commodities: truth, righteousness, faith, the gospel, God's Word, and prayer. They are not cryptic formulas, but the simple assets every believer inherits in Christ.

How can we use those weapons? Technique is not the issue; personal character is. Look once again at 1 Timothy 1:18–19. Paul says, "Timothy, my son . . . fight the good fight, *keeping faith and a good conscience*" (emphasis added). That sheds some light on how we are to fight the devil. Rather than chasing demons around, trying to figure out their names and shooing them away, Paul told Timothy to focus on keeping the faith (sound doctrine) and a clear conscience (righteous living so the conscience cannot accuse).

Again, in 2 Timothy 2:3–4, Paul writes, "Suffer hardship with me, as a good soldier of Christ Jesus. No soldier in active service entangles himself in the affairs of everyday life, so that he may please the one who enlisted him as a soldier." Here's another very crucial principle for success in the war against the powers of darkness: disentangle yourself from worldly things, and commit yourself to doing the will of the Commander.

Do you see what Scripture is saying? If we do not use the truth, live the truth, believe the truth—if we do not have clear consciences that come from holy living, and if we are not disentangled from the world, doing the will of God— it doesn't matter what we *say* to the powers of darkness. Winning against Satan is not a question of claiming some kind of imagined authority over him; we simply need to pursue righteousness, avoid sin, and stand firm in the truth. Satan cannot defeat any believer who lives that way. Conversely, weak doctrine and sinful living will make a person vulnerable no matter what verbiage he may spit into the air thinking Satan is listening.

First Peter 5:9 is as straightforward as possible. Satan walks around like a devouring lion, the apostle says. What are we to do? "Resist him." How can we do that? Peter gives no formula. He doesn't say, "Bind him." He's not talking about that kind of resistance. He says simply, "Resist him, firm in your faith." James 4:7 offers the same strategy: "Submit therefore to God. Resist the devil and he will flee from you."

This is not a complex battle plan: Submit to God and resist the devil. How? By being firm in the faith, committed to truth, and keeping a clear conscience. What will Satan's response be? "He will flee from you." That is the only statement in all the New Testament that tells us how to get rid of Satan. There are no biblical guidelines for exorcism. There is no more elaborate strategy for spiritual warfare. There is nothing in Scripture that tells a believer to speak to demons, cast them out, bind them, tie them up, or do anything like that.

When Jesus was tempted by the devil, He didn't mock him, condemn him, bind him, send him to the pit, or stomp on his neck. He simply said, "It is written," then quoted a portion of Scripture that specifically addressed each temptation (Matt. 4:1–11; Luke 4:1–13). He withstood the devil simply through the power and authority of God's Word. That was the only means our Lord used to conquer Satan. He resisted, and Satan fled. It should be noted that even that encounter was the will of God, as Jesus was led to it by the Holy Spirit (Matt. 4:1).

You might be interested to learn that there is no illustration in the entire Bible of anyone casting demons out of a believer. The only people who ever legitimately cast out demons were Christ and the apostles. All the demon-possessed people they dealt with were unbelievers. Furthermore, they usually cast out demons totally apart from the will of the unbeliever. Jesus and the Twelve were exercising the gift of miracles. They were authenticating messianic and apostolic credentials, not establishing a pattern for us to follow.

Our instructions for fighting Satan are only to resist him, being strong in the faith, with a clear conscience and a commitment to truth and holiness. It is as simple as this: If there is sin in your life or if you tolerate error, you give place to Satan. If you are strong in the faith and resist, he will flee (James 4:7, see also 1 John 2:14).

One night several years ago I was called to the church office to deal with an emergency. I arrived to find one of our elders struggling with a girl who was demon possessed. She was evidencing supernatural strength; she had flipped a heavy steel desk over onto its top. The two of us together were unable to restrain her physically. Voices that were not her own were speaking out of her. I was unsure of what to do, having never encountered anything like that before.

When I arrived, I heard a demon scream, "Not *him!* Anyone but *him!* Get him out! Get him out! We don't want him here." It encouraged me to know they realized I was not on their side.

We tried to speak to the demons. We commanded them to tell us their names, and we ordered them in Jesus' name to go to the pit. We spent two hours trying to send those demons out of her.

When we finally stopped trying to talk to the demons and dealt directly with that young woman, we began to make some headway. We told her she needed to confess her sins, and she began to pour out her heart. She had been involved in unimaginable filth and was living a hypocritical life. She confessed her sins with tears and affirmed the truth of Jesus Christ, then asked the Lord to cleanse her from every sin in her life. Again in her prayer, she articulated every sin she could think of having committed and prayed earnestly with a repentant heart. Afterward she was a changed woman. As far as I know, demons have never troubled her from that day on.

How was she delivered? Not by any spectacular deliverance ceremony. She simply resisted the demons with truth and righteousness, and they fled.

There's no question that Christianity is a spiritual battle with the forces of evil. But our weapons are not fleshly; they're not secret; they're not so complex that we need a seminar to teach us how to use them. They're part of the wealth that is ours in our all-sufficient Savior.

11

Sufficient Grace

He has said to me, "My grace is sufficient for you, for power is perfected in weakness." Most gladly, therefore, I will rather boast about my weaknesses, that the power of Christ may dwell in me.

2 Corinthians 12:9

A POOR MAN HAD WANTED TO GO ON A CRUISE all his life. As a youngster he had seen an advertisement for a luxury cruise, and ever since, he had dreamed of spending a week on a large ocean liner enjoying fresh sea air and relaxing in a luxurious environment. He saved money for years, carefully counting his pennies, often sacrificing personal needs so he could stretch his resources a little further.

Finally he had enough to purchase a cruise ticket. He went to a travel agent, looked over the cruise brochures, picked out one that was especially attractive, and bought a ticket with the money he had saved so long. He was hardly able to believe he was about to realize his childhood dream.

Knowing he could not afford the kind of elegant food pictured in the brochure, the man planned to bring his own provisions for the week. Accustomed to moderation after years of frugal living, and with his entire savings going to pay for the cruise ticket, the man decided to bring along a week's supply of bread and peanut butter. That was all he could afford.

The first few days of the cruise were thrilling. The man ate peanut-butter sandwiches alone in his room each morning and spent the rest of his time relaxing in the sunlight and fresh air, delighted to be aboard ship.

By midweek, however, the man was beginning to notice that he was the only person on board who was not eating luxurious meals. It seemed that every time he sat on the deck or rested in the lounge or stepped outside his cabin, a porter would walk by with a huge meal for someone who had ordered room service.

By the fifth day of the cruise the man could take it no longer. The peanut-butter sandwiches seemed stale and tasteless. He was desperately hungry, and even the fresh air and sunshine had lost their appeal. Finally, he stopped a porter and exclaimed, "Tell me how I might get one of those meals! I'm dying for some decent food, and I'll do anything you say to earn it!"

"Why, sir, don't you have a ticket for this cruise?" the porter asked.

"Certainly," said the man. "But I spent everything I had for that ticket. I have nothing left with which to buy food."

"But sir," said the porter, "didn't you realize? Meals are included with your passage. You may eat as much as you like!"

Lots of Christians live like that man. Not realizing the unlimited provisions that are theirs in Christ, they munch on stale scraps. There's no need to live like that! Everything we could ever want or need is included in the cost of admission—and the Savior has already paid it for us!

There's a single word that encompasses all the riches we find in Christ: *grace*. What a magnificent word it is! It is used more than 150 times in the New Testament to speak of divine favor bestowed on undeserving people. It is the means by which we receive every physical and spiritual benefit.

To some measure even unbelievers benefit from God's grace. Theologians call that "common grace" because it is common to all mankind. Common grace is God's continual care for all creation, providing for his creatures' needs. Through common grace God restrains humanity from utter debauchery and maintains order and some sense of beauty, morality, and goodness in society's consciousness.

Christians, however, receive a greater grace (James 4:6). To us God's grace is inexhaustible and boundless, including all that we have talked about regarding the all-sufficient provisions of Jesus Christ.

We are saved by grace (Eph. 2:8) and in grace we stand (Rom. 5:2). Grace upholds our salvation, gives us victory in temptation, and helps us endure suffering and pain. It helps us understand the Word and wisely apply it to our lives. It draws us into communion and prayer and enables us to serve the Lord effectively. In short, we exist and are firmly fixed in an environment of all-sufficient grace.

Grace upon Grace

One of the most wonderful statements about our Lord is that He was "full of grace" (John 1:14) and "of His fulness have all we received and grace upon grace" (John 1:16). "Grace upon grace" speaks of accumulated grace—one grace following upon another. Such grace is ours each day. It is unlimited and sufficient for every need. Paul called it "the abundance of grace" (Rom. 5:17), "the riches of [God's] grace" (Eph. 2:7), and "surpassing grace" (2 Cor. 9:14). Peter called it the "manifold" (in Greek, *poikilos*, "multifaceted" or "multicolored") grace of God (1 Pet. 4:10). He used the same Greek word in 1 Peter 1:6 with reference to the various trials that believers face. That's a wonderful parallel: God's multifaceted grace is sufficient for our multifaceted trials.

Super-Abounding Grace

Perhaps nowhere is the magnificence of grace more wonderfully stated than in 2 Corinthians 9:8–11. The superlatives here are staggering: "God is able to make *all* grace *abound* to you, that *always* having *all* sufficiency in *everything*, you may have an *abundance* for *every* good deed. . . . You will be enriched in *everything* for *all* liberality, which through us is producing thanksgiving to God" (emphasis added).

In a sense, that one verse sums up everything that could ever be said about our sufficiency in Christ. Set in a context describing God's material provision, these verses have meaning that obviously extends to limitless proportions. Surpassing grace indwells every believer (v. 14). Is it any wonder Paul could not restrain his praise to God for such an indescribable gift (v. 15)?

All-Sufficient Grace

Paul experienced God's grace as few others have because he endured suffering as few others have. In

2 Corinthians 12:9 the Lord gave him one of the most profound truths in all revelation: "My grace is sufficient for you, for power is perfected in weakness." That wonderful promise extends to every believer, but its context is one of severe difficulties, distresses, persecutions, and human weaknesses (v. 10).

Second Corinthians 10 through 13 is probably the most emotionally charged text Paul ever wrote. In it he pours out his heart amid severe attacks on his character and ministry. He had given so much to the Corinthians, and some of them were turning on him with bitter animosity. His integrity had been called into question by his enemies. His loyalty and leadership abilities had been questioned. His love for believers had been doubted and denied. This was probably the greatest single barrage of abuse that Paul ever received in his life—and apparently it was being fueled by leaders within the church.

In chapter 11 Paul chronicles many of the hardships and life-threatening situations he had endured. Included in his list are great physical trials—imprisonments, beatings, stonings, shipwrecks, dangerous rivers, robbers, Jewish and Gentile persecutions, sleepless nights, inclement weather, and lack of food and drink (vv. 23–27). More painful than all that was the daily concern he had for all the churches (v. 28). God's people and His church were Paul's greatest passion (Col. 1:28–29) and presented the highest potential for pain and disappointment.

The greatest pain he ever knew came from some of the people he loved the most—those to whom he had given his soul and his gospel, but who now had turned against him. Their rejection, betrayal, criticism, false accusations, and even hatred cut deep into his heart. In

2 Corinthians he wrote as a man who was unloved, unappreciated, distrusted, and deeply troubled in his soul.

Perhaps you can relate to Paul's deep hurt. People were created for relationships—first with God, then with other human beings. When relationships fail, the fallout can be severe, as evidenced in our society by the ever-increasing number of people seeking professional psychiatric help for rejection and emotional abuse similar to what Paul experienced. That makes Paul's situation very practical to us because the same pain that hit him can strike every believer.

The Lessons of Grace

Paul's distressing circumstances put him in a position to learn some marvelous lessons about God's grace, which he passes on to us in 2 Corinthians 12:7–10:

> Because of the surpassing greatness of the revelations, for this reason, to keep me from exalting myself, there was given me a thorn in the flesh, a messenger of Satan to buffet me—to keep me from exalting myself! Concerning this I entreated the Lord three times that it might depart from me. And He has said to me, "My grace is sufficient for you, for power is perfected in weakness." Most gladly, therefore, I will rather boast about my weaknesses, that the power of Christ may dwell in me. Therefore I am well content with weaknesses, with insults, with distresses, with persecutions, with difficulties, for Christ's sake; for when I am weak, then I am strong.

Humility. God knows that men are prone toward pride, especially when they are in positions of spiritual privilege. Therefore He often uses opposition and suffering to teach them humility.

Paul was perhaps the most spiritually privileged man who ever lived, and the Lord's grace in his life was abundant. On at least four occasions Jesus Himself appeared to him to instruct or encourage him in times of deep need (Acts 9:4–6; 18:9–10; 22:17–21; 23:11; 2 Cor. 12:1–4). He received such extensive divine revelation that his writings amount to nearly half of the New Testament books.

Because of the extraordinary nature of those revelations, God gave Paul a "thorn in the flesh" to keep him from exalting himself (2 Cor. 12:7). That phrase might elicit a picture of cutting roses and having a little thorn stick your finger. But as we noted in the previous chapter, the Greek word translated "thorn" literally means a stake—a sharpened wooden shaft used to impale or torture someone. Further, the phrase "in the flesh" can also be rendered "for the flesh," which I believe is the better rendering here. Metaphorically speaking, God gave Paul a stake for his sinful flesh to impale and kill it so as to prevent boasting and pride.

Paul described the thorn as "a messenger of Satan" (v. 7). There are many differing views of what that means, but if we take it at face value, we can simplify the issue greatly. A messenger of Satan is someone whom Satan sends with a message—that's clear enough. The Greek word translated "messenger" is *angelos,* which is used more than 188 times in the New Testament and always refers to a person—either human or angelic. Therefore it is highly unlikely that Paul was using it in verse 7 to refer to a physical ailment, as many commentators suggest. Simply stated, Paul's thorn in the flesh was a person, and I'm convinced it was the ringleader of the Corinthian opposition who was discrediting Paul by personally attacking his character and ministry—and turning people Paul loved against him.

In 2 Corinthians 11:13–15 Paul says that those in Corinth who opposed the gospel were "false apostles, deceitful workers, disguising themselves as apostles of Christ. And no wonder, for even Satan disguises himself as an angel of light. Therefore it is not surprising if his servants also disguise themselves as servants of righteousness; whose end shall be according to their deeds." Satan has his demonic forces, but that passage speaks of men (v. 13) whom he sends out disguised as messengers of truth who attempt to deceive and damn people through false teaching (vv. 3–4).

In Paul's case, this messenger was sent to buffet or torment him (v. 7). "Buffet" literally means "to strike with the fist" or "beat." It is used in Matthew 26:67 and Mark 14:65 of the Roman soldiers who punched Jesus in the face. In 1 Corinthians 4:11 it speaks of Paul's being "roughly treated."

Paul's point is that God moved Satan to dispatch someone to aggressively abuse him. As we saw in the previous chapter, Paul understood this; he even knew the reason for it: "to keep me from exalting myself!" (v. 7). That is, just as He had used Satan to humble Job and Peter, God was preparing Paul for greater usefulness. Unlike many human counselors who try to elevate a person's opinion of himself, God will deflate us so we see our proper relationship to Him. Then He will exalt us according to His will and give us abundant grace (James 4:6, 10).

Dependence. Often other believers are channels of God's grace, but He alone is its source. We tend to turn to people with our hurts, but God wants us to look to Him first of all in times of trouble.

That was Paul's response. In 2 Corinthians 12:8 he says, "Concerning this I entreated the Lord three times that [my thorn in the flesh] might depart from me." To entreat is to ask or appeal to someone. Please note that he doesn't say, "Concerning this I went to my therapist, attended a seminar, read a book, or rebuked Satan." He took a route many today feel is too simplistic—he entreated the Lord!

Three times he appealed to God to remove the thorn—three times the Lord said no. Paul prayed persistently and faithfully, yet he learned that God's purposes could be better accomplished by the answer no.

Sufficiency. Paul was content with God's decision because he knew that God would supply sufficient grace for his trial. "He has said to me, 'My grace is sufficient for you'" (v. 9). "He has said" is in the perfect tense in the Greek text, implying that every time Paul prayed, God said the same thing and kept on saying it. "My grace is sufficient for you" was his standing answer. After three times, Paul dropped the request.

God answered Paul's prayer, not by giving him what he asked, not by removing the problem or pain, but by supplying sufficient grace for Paul to endure it. Why remove something that generates such immense benefits as humility, communion, and increased glory to God?

Like Paul, we might ask God to remove some stake of suffering, only to discover that God wants it to remain. Yielding to His will at such times is the cornerstone of Christian living. Troubles, temptations, and pain are inevitable in this life. But remember that God uses them to produce the precious fruit of humility, fellowship, and glory.

He may not remove them, but He has promised sufficient grace to enable us to endure them with joy.

Power. The same suffering that reveals our weaknesses reveals God's strength, "for power is perfected in weakness" (v. 9). When we are least effective in our human strength and have only God's power to sustain us, then we are suitable channels through which His power flows. And so we should praise God for adversity because that's when His power is most evident in our lives. There is no one too weak to be powerful, but there are many too strong.

Paul understood that. His attitude was one of joy and praise. In verse 9 he says, "Most gladly, therefore, I will rather boast about my weaknesses, that the power of Christ may dwell in me." He wasn't a masochist. He didn't love abuse, but he loved the grace and power that God manifested in him. He knew that spiritual ministry can be accomplished only in the power of the Spirit. When his reputation was gone, he couldn't rely on that. When his physical strength was spent, he couldn't lean on that. He was reduced to preaching the message God had entrusted to him and relying on God's power to do the rest—and God never failed him.

Contentment. Paul gives us a key principle in verse 10: "Therefore I am well content with weaknesses, with insults, with distresses, with persecutions, and with difficulties, for Christ's sake; for when I am weak, then I am strong." Paul embraced his deepest trouble as a friend to lead him to greater spiritual usefulness.

What a contrast that is to our society! Most people are discontent because they wrongly equate satisfaction with positive circumstances and increased possessions. Many Christians seem to think that sheltering believers from all difficulties is the highest expression of God's grace. The so-called prosperity gospel—the philosophical offspring of our self-centered, godless society—is a major contributor to that error.

In that regard, Michael Horton has written:

> It is appropriate that a prosperity gospel be born in the hedonistic, self-centered, get-rich-quick milieu of modern American society. We are, by nature, pagan. Either our religion will transform us or we will transform our religion to suit our sympathies. . . .
>
> The prosperity Bible does not deal only with freedom from sickness. It would have us read, "He Himself bore our sickness *and poverty* in His body on the tree, so that we might die to *infirmity* and *lack*; for by His wounds you have been healed." In contrast, there was no question in the mind of the apostles that the gospel promised "spiritual riches in heavenly places in Christ" (Ephesians 1:3), not earthly ones. Our Lord was afflicted so that we could be healed. But that is a metaphor for the wonderful truth that the penalty justly meant for us was endured instead by Christ, our substitute. The rod of justice that dealt the Lamb of God such bitter blows declared *us* righteous!
>
> It is to trivialize greatly the work of Christ to suggest that God the Father sent His only-begotten Son into the world to bear the world's blasphemy, insults, and violence, and, most of all, to bear the Father's wrath—all for increased cash flow and fewer bouts with asthma. It is to make a joke out of the great displeasure, anger, and wrath God has toward sin and sinful persons. God's real problem, say the faith teachers, is not that we are wicked, selfish, God-hating rebels who deserve eternal punishment, but that we aren't enjoying ourselves! (emphasis in original)[1]

251

That kind of thinking breeds spiritual poverty, not prosperity. It does violence to God's grace and replaces true spiritual riches with greed and disillusionment. It leaves people feeling abandoned by God or questioning their faith when difficulties come. It impugns the integrity of Jesus, who said that a disciple isn't above his teacher or a servant above his master (Matt. 10:24); of Peter, who said that we were called for the purpose of suffering, since Jesus suffered for us and left us an example to follow (1 Pet. 2:21); of Paul, who said that all believers will experience persecution (2 Tim. 3:12); and of James, who said that trials produce spiritual maturity (James 1:2–4).

The apostle instructed the Colossians, "Walk in a manner worthy of the Lord . . . strengthened with all power, according to His glorious might, for the attaining of all steadfastness and patience; joyously giving thanks to the Father, who has qualified us to share in the inheritance of the saints in light" (Col. 1:10–12). "Strengthened with all power"! For what? Health, wealth, prosperity, healings, miracles, signs, and wonders? No. "For the attaining of all steadfastness and patience"—things necessary in times of trouble. This is no promise of trouble-free living, only power to endure the trouble that is inevitable. How are we to endure it? "Joyously giving thanks to the Father" for an eternal inheritance, not temporal riches.

Grace Amid Trials

God has always used suffering to perfect and purify His people and to demonstrate the sufficiency of His grace. It's only when we don't trust in His sovereignty or don't understand His purposes, that we are apt to experience worry, fear, and anxiety when things go wrong. But suffering brings enormous benefits:

Suffering Verifies Our Faith. Peter used the analogy of an assayer or goldsmith to illustrate this benefit of suffering. Just as a goldsmith uses fire to purify gold by burning away the dross, so God uses trials to test and to purify our faith:

> [You] are protected by the power of God through faith for a salvation ready to be revealed in the last time. In this you greatly rejoice, even though now for a little while, if necessary, you have been distressed by various trials, that the proof of your faith, being more precious than gold which is perishable, even though tested by fire, may be found to result in praise and glory and honor at the revelation of Jesus Christ. (1 Pet. 1:6–7)

Those verses tell us that trials are temporary ("for a little while"); they bring both physical and mental anguish ("you have been distressed"); they come in many forms ("by various trials"); but they needn't diminish our joy ("in this you greatly rejoice").

"Fire" symbolizes trials, "gold" symbolizes our faith, and "proof" is the final product of the purifying process—the tested, pure metal. A proven faith is precious because it gives us the joy and assurance of knowing we are genuine Christians.

Suffering Confirms Our Sonship. Even when your suffering is the result of God's chastening, you can rejoice because it proves that He loves you. Hebrews 12:5–8 says,

> "My son, do not regard lightly the discipline of the
>   Lord,
> Nor faint when you are reproved by Him;

For those whom the Lord loves He disciplines,
And He scourges every son whom He receives."
It is for discipline that you endure; God deals with
you as with sons; for what son is there whom his father
does not discipline? But if you are without discipline,
of which all have become partakers, then you are ille-
gitimate children and not sons.

Suffering Produces Endurance. James said, "Consider it
all joy, my brethren, when you encounter various trials,
knowing that the testing of your faith produces endurance.
And let endurance have its perfect result, that you may be
perfect and complete, lacking in nothing" (James 1:2–4).

First Peter 5:10 says, "After you have suffered for a
little while, the God of all grace, who called you to His
eternal glory in Christ, will Himself perfect, confirm,
strengthen and establish you."

Suffering Teaches Us to Hate Sin. The imprecatory
psalms are David's cry for God's vengeance on his enemies.
After enduring much suffering, Martin Luther admitted that
he had gained a fondness for those particular psalms. Suffering taught him to share David's hatred of sin.

When Jesus saw Mary weeping over the death of her
beloved brother Lazarus, He was "deeply moved in spirit,
and was troubled" (John 11:33). He was angry at the pain
and sorrow that sin had inflicted on Lazarus's family.

Suffering Promotes Self-Evaluation. When circumstances are good, it's easy to praise the Lord and feel opti-
mistic about life in general. When troubles come, we often
become impatient with God and question His sovereignty
and grace. At such times we are forced to look deep into
our hearts and deal with our lack of faith. They can be precious times of profound spiritual discovery and growth.

Suffering Clarifies Our Priorities. In times of prosperity, our hearts can be divided and our priorities confused. God warned the Israelites to guard against that when they entered the Promised Land (Deut. 6:10–13). When suffering comes, it changes our focus from the world to God.

Suffering Identifies Us with Christ. Suffering for the Lord's sake is a distinguishing mark of all true believers. Paul told Timothy that "all who desire to live godly in Christ Jesus will be persecuted" (2 Tim. 3:12). He said to the Thessalonian believers, "You, brethren, became imitators of the churches of God in Christ Jesus that are in Judea, for you also endured the same sufferings at the hand of your own countrymen, even as they did from the Jews, who both killed the Lord Jesus and the prophets, and drove us out" (1 Thess. 2:14–15).

In Galatians 6:17 Paul says, "I bear on my body the brand-marks of Jesus." He received wounds that were aimed at Christ. It was his privilege to do so because he longed to share in the fellowship of Christ's suffering (Phil. 3:10).

Suffering Can Encourage Other Believers. Often God uses the suffering of one believer to encourage and strengthen others. The response of the Thessalonian Christians to their trials was an example to believers throughout all Macedonia and Achaia (1 Thess. 1:6–7). Paul's first imprisonment resulted in greater progress for the gospel because it gave other believers "far more courage to speak the word of God without fear" (Phil. 1:14).

Suffering Can Benefit Unbelievers. Many unbelievers are elect individuals who have not yet been redeemed. Quite often the Lord uses the persecution of believers to draw the elect to Himself—like He did with the Philippian jailer in Acts 16. The jailer was charged with guarding Paul and Silas after they had been beaten unlawfully and thrown into prison. Their only "crimes" were proclaiming Christ and casting an evil spirit out of a slave-girl (vv. 16–23).

The jailer surely heard them praying and singing hymns of praise to God (v. 25) because following the miraculous earthquake in verse 26, and his near suicide in verse 27, he asked them what he had to do to be saved (v. 30). Paul and Silas preached the gospel to him and his entire household, and they all believed (vv. 31–34).

Suffering Enables Us to Help Others. Often those who suffer the most are most sensitive to the suffering of others. That promotes the wonderful graces of mercy and compassion. In a sense, that's the thrust of Hebrews 4:15–16: "We do not have a high priest who cannot sympathize with our weaknesses, but one who has been tempted in all things as we are, yet without sin. Let us therefore draw near with confidence to the throne of grace, that we may receive mercy and may find grace to help in time of need."

Jesus knows how much we struggle with temptation and human frailties because He had similar struggles. He can sympathize with us and comfort us as we draw near to Him through prayer and the Word.

God's grace is more than sufficient for your every need. Is your relationship with Him deep and trusting enough to draw you to Him during times of difficulty? Are you content to endure weaknesses, insults, distresses, and persecutions for Christ's sake so that you can be spiritually strong even amid physical and emotional weakness?

The story is told of Charles Haddon Spurgeon, who was riding home one evening after a heavy day's work, feeling weary and depressed, when the verse came to mind, "My grace is sufficient for you."

In his mind he immediately compared himself to a little fish in the Thames River, apprehensive lest drinking so many pints of water in the river each day he might drink the Thames dry. Then Father Thames says to him, "Drink away, little fish. My stream is sufficient for you."

Next he thought of a little mouse in the granaries of Egypt, afraid lest its daily nibbles exhaust the supplies and cause it to starve to death. Then Joseph comes along and says, "Cheer up, little mouse. My granaries are sufficient for you."

Then he thought of a man climbing some high mountain to reach its lofty summit and dreading lest his breathing there might exhaust all the oxygen in the atmosphere. The Creator booms His voice out of heaven, saying, "Breathe away, oh man, and fill your lungs. My atmosphere is sufficient for you!"

Let us rest in the abundance of God's wonderful grace and the total sufficiency of all His spiritual resources. That's the all-sufficient Savior's legacy to His people.

"May grace and peace be yours in fullest measure" (1 Pet. 1:2)!

12

Epilogue: Perfect Sufficiency

Walk in a manner worthy of the Lord, to please Him in all respects, bearing fruit in every good work and increasing in the knowledge of God; strengthened with all power, according to His glorious might, for the attaining of all steadfastness and patience; joyously giving thanks to the Father, who has qualified us to share in the inheritance of the saints in light.

Colossians 1:10–12

Not that we are adequate in ourselves to consider anything as coming from ourselves, but our adequacy is from God.

2 Corinthians 3:5

AS CHRISTIANS, WE LIVE AT A STRATA FOR which human wisdom cannot provide resources. Our ability to live the Christian life is from God alone. And when it comes to spiritual matters, all we need to know is revealed in God's Word and ministered to us by His Spirit. We needn't look elsewhere.

One of the Old Testament names of God is *El Shaddai*, meaning "the All-Sufficient One." It is a name rich with meaning. Those who worship Him in Spirit and in truth find Him adequate for every necessity of life. They do not need any supplementary experience, a stronger dose of His redemption, or any other spiritual or emotional accoutrements. God has given to every believer abundant grace that is utterly sufficient to fulfill our deepest longings, our most intense cravings, our most profound needs—every human requirement.

I recently searched through my library, looking for information on one attribute of God—His generosity. I was amazed to discover that almost nothing has been written on the subject. I didn't find it listed in any systematic theology. It wasn't in any of the texts on the character and attributes of God. I couldn't find it anywhere. I spent an entire afternoon reading indexes, trying to find something that has been written about God's generosity. Have Christian theologians perhaps questioned whether God is really very generous? Do we suspect that He is stingy?

Of course He's not. In Exodus 34:6 God gives Moses a first-person assessment of His own character. This is what He says: "[I] The Lord, the Lord God, [am] compassionate and gracious, slow to anger, and abounding in lovingkindness and truth." Lamentations 3:22–23 says, "The Lord's lovingkindnesses indeed never cease, / For His compassions never fail. / They are new every morning; / Great is Thy faithfulness." Those verses and scores of others like them show that God's generosity is endless—and it's most abundant when He is disbursing lovingkindness and mercy. His compassions never fail; His faithfulness is great; His grace is sufficient.

How generous is God? Romans 8:32 says, "He who did not spare His own Son, but delivered Him up for us all, how will He not also with Him freely give us all things?" That's simple logic: Since God has already given us His best—His own Son—why would He not give us everything else that's good? He has given us the highest and best; would He hold out from giving us lesser things? Not at all.

John 1:16 says, "Of His fulness we have all received, and grace upon grace." When we receive Christ, we get everything we need. That's why He came—to provide life, and that more abundantly (John 10:10).

Paul wrote to the struggling church at Corinth, "All things belong to you" (1 Cor. 3:21). He wanted even those fragmented believers to know that their sufficiency was in Christ. Rather than fighting among themselves, taking sides against their brethren, they needed to step back and survey the riches that were theirs in Christ. There was no reason to battle one another. There was no need to give in to pride, sin, and false doctrine. They were equipped by Christ Himself with all they could ever need.

The church today desperately needs to embrace that message. Christians today are consumed with the trials and troubles of life. They are caught up with difficulties and sorrows and anguish. And they are desperately looking for some great new secret, some higher spiritual level, some more effective relief than they think they have in Christ. Consequently the church is fragmented and severely weakened.

There's no need for that. His grace is sufficient. He has blessed us with every spiritual blessing. We are partakers of the divine nature. Christ lives in us. We are blessed in Him with all we could ever need.

Is there sufficiency in Christ? Absolute sufficiency. The challenge for us is to know Him better, to serve Him more fervently, and to be more conformed to His image. Paul told the Ephesians his prayer for them was that they might "be able to comprehend with all the saints what is the breadth and length and height and depth, and to know the love of Christ which surpasses knowledge, that you may be filled up to all the fulness of God" (Eph. 3:18–19).

My prayer is that you won't exchange the fountain of life from which flow rivers of living water for the broken pots being sold today—which hold no water.

For My people have committed two evils:
They have forsaken Me,
The fountain of living waters,
To hew for themselves cisterns,
Broken cisterns,
That can hold no water.

Jeremiah 2:13

ENDNOTES

Preface

1. C. S. Lewis, *The Screwtape Letters* (New York: Macmillan, 1961), pp. 126–30. Used by permission of Harper Collins Press.

Chapter 3 Does God Need a Psychiatrist?

1. *Time*, 2 April 1979, p. 74.
2. Ibid., p. 79.
3. Ibid.
4. Ibid., p. 82.
5. Ann Japenga, "Great Minds on the Mind Assemble for Conference," *Los Angeles Times*, 18 December 1985, p. V1.
6. Ibid., p. V17.
7. "A Therapist in Every Corner," *Time*, 23 December 1985, p. 59.
8. Ibid.
9. Japenga, p. 16.
10. *Time*, 23 December 1985, p. 59.
11. Japenga, 16.
12. Nicole Brodeur, "Center Aids Christian Sex Addicts," *Orange County Register*, 13 February 1989, p. 1.
13. Ibid.
14. Ibid.

Chapter 4 Truth in a World of Theory

1. Albert Barnes, *Notes on the Old Testament: Psalms*, vol. 1 (Grand Rapids: Baker, 1974), p. 171.
2. Samuel Cox, cited in Marvin Vincent, *Word Studies in the New Testament: II Peter* (Grand Rapids: Eerdmans, 1980), p. 687.
3. Priscilla Slagle, *The Way Up from Down* (New York: Random House, 1987), pp. 218–27.

Chapter 5 Psychological Sanctification?

1. John F. MacArthur, Jr., *Hebrews* (Chicago: Moody, 1983), p. 91.
2. *The New Testament in Modern English,* revised edition, translated by J. B. Phillips (New York: Macmillan, 1972).
3. *The Jerusalem Bible* (Garden City: Doubleday, 1968).

Chapter 6 Bible-Believing Doubters

1. J. I. Packer, *God Has Spoken: Revelation and the Bible* (London: Hodder and Stoughton, 1965), pp. 11–12.
2. Richard Trench, *Synonyms of the New Testament* (Grand Rapids: Eerdmans, 1983), p. 13.
3. Robert Thomas, "Precision as God's Will for My Life" pamphlet (Panorama City, Calif.: The Master's Seminary, 1989).
4. Ibid.
5. Robert L. Reymond, *Preach the Word! A Teaching Ministry Approved unto God* (Edinburgh: Rutherford House, 1988), pp. 84–85.
6. Charles H. Spurgeon, *The Metropolitan Tabernacle Pulpit,* vol. XXXII (Pasadena, Texas: Pilgrim Publications, 1986), pp. 385–86.

Chapter 7 Religious Hedonism

1. Harry Emerson Fosdick, "What Is the Matter with Preaching?" *Harpers Magazine* (July 1928), pp. 134–35.
2. Ibid.
3. Ibid., p. 138.
4. Robert Schuller, *Self-Esteem: The New Reformation* (Waco, Texas: Word, 1982), p. 12.
5. Ibid., p. 31.
6. Walter Chantry, *Today's Gospel: Authentic or Synthetic?* (Edinburgh: Banner of Truth, 1970), pp. 25–26.
7. Iain Murray, *D. Martyn Lloyd-Jones: The Fight of Faith* (Edinburgh: Banner of Truth, 1990), p. 327.
8. Tony Walter, *Need: The New Religion* (Downer's Grove: Intervarsity, 1985), preface, p. 5.
9. John F. MacArthur, Jr., *1 Corinthians* (Chicago: Moody, 1984), p. 213.

Chapter 8 The Quest for Something More

1. Adolf Schlatter, as cited in F. F. Bruce, *The Epistles to the Colossians, to Philemon, and to the Ephesians* (Grand Rapids: Eerdmans, 1984), p. 98.
2. Flavius Josephus, *The Jewish Wars* II. viii. 2.
3. Arthur Johnson, *Faith Misguided: Exposing the Dangers of Mysticism* (Chicago: Moody, 1988), pp. 20–23.

Chapter 10 Spiritual Warfare: Who's After Whom?

1. John Dart, "Evangelicals, Charismatics Prepare for Spiritual Warfare," *Los Angeles Times*, 17 February 1990, p. F16.
2. John F. MacArthur, Jr., *Ephesians* (Chicago: Moody, 1985), pp. 345–85.

Chapter 11 Sufficient Grace

1. Michael Horton, *The Agony of Deceit* (Chicago: Moody, 1990), pp. 123–25.

TOPICAL INDEX

SCRIPTURE INDEX